FLAT STANLEY

His Original Adventure!

Flat Stanley: His Original Adventure!
Text copyright © 1964 by Jeff Brown
Copyright renewed © 1992 by Jeff Brown
Illustrations by Macky Pamintuan, copyright © 2009 by HarperCollins Publishers
All rights reserved.

Published in agreement with the author, c/o BAROR INTERNATIONAL, INC., Armonk, New York, U.S.A. through Danny Hong Agency, Seoul, Korea.

ISBN 979-11-91343-59-5 14740

Longtail Books

FLAT STANLEY

His Original Adventure!

by Jeff Brown
Pictures by Macky Pamintuan

For J.C. and Tony
—J.B.

CONTENTS

The Big Bulletin Board

Breakfast was ready.

"I will go wake the boys," Mrs. Lambchop said to her husband, George Lambchop. Just then their younger son, Arthur, called from the bedroom he shared with his brother, Stanley.

"Hey! Come and look! Hey!"

Mr. and Mrs. Lambchop were both

very much in **favor** of **polite**ness and careful speech. "**Hay** is for horses, Arthur, not people," Mr. Lambchop said as they entered the bedroom. "Try to remember that."

"Excuse me," Arthur said. "But look!"

He pointed to Stanley's bed. Across it lay the **enormous** bulletin board that Mr. Lambchop had given the boys a Christmas ago so that they could **pin** up pictures and messages and maps. It had fallen, during the night, on top of Stanley.

But Stanley was not hurt. In fact, he would still have been sleeping if he had not been woken by his brother's shout.

"What's going on here?" he called out **cheerful**ly from **beneath** the enormous board.

Mr. and Mrs. Lambchop hurried to lift it from the bed.

"**Heavens**!" said Mrs. Lambchop.

"**Gosh**!" said Arthur. "Stanley's flat!"

"As a pancake," said Mr. Lambchop.

"Darndest* thing I've ever seen."

"Let's all have breakfast," Mrs. Lambchop said. "Then Stanley and I will go see Dr. Dan and hear what he has to say."

In his office, Dr. Dan **examine**d Stanley all over.

"How do you feel?" he asked. "Does it hurt very much?"

"I felt sort of **tickly** for a while after I got up," Stanley Lambchop said, "but I feel fine now."

"Well, that's mostly how it is with these **case**s," said Dr. Dan.

"We'll just have to **keep an eye on**

★ **darndest** '몹시 놀라운' 또는 '터무니없는'이라는 뜻의 'damnedest'를 순화한 표현.

this young **fellow**," he said when he had finished the examination. "Sometimes we doctors, despite all our years of training and experience, can only **marvel** at how little we really know."

Mrs. Lambchop said she thought Stanley's clothes would have to be **alter**ed by the **tailor** now, so Dr. Dan told his nurse to take Stanley's **measure**ments.

Mrs. Lambchop wrote them down.

Stanley was four feet* tall, about a foot wide, and half an inch* thick.

★ **feet** 길이의 단위 피트. 1피트는 약 30.48센티미터이다.
⁑ **inch** 길이의 단위 인치. 1인치는 약 2.54센티미터이다.

Being Flat

When Stanley **got used to** being flat, he
enjoyed it. He could go in and out of
rooms, even when the door was closed,
just by lying down and **sliding** through
the **crack** at the bottom.

Mr. and Mrs. Lambchop said it was
silly, but they were quite proud of him.

Arthur got **jealous** and tried to slide

under a door, but he just **bang**ed his head.

Being flat could also be **helpful**, Stanley found.

He was taking a walk with Mrs. Lambchop one afternoon when her favorite ring fell from her finger. The ring **roll**ed across the **sidewalk** and down between the **bar**s of a **grating** that **cover**ed a deep, dark **shaft**. Mrs. Lambchop began to cry.

"I have an idea," Stanley said.

He took the **lace**s out of his shoes and an **extra** pair out of his pocket and **tie**d them all together to make one long lace. Then he tied one end of that to the back of his belt and gave the other end to his mother.

"**Lower** me," he said, "and I will look for the ring."

"Thank you, Stanley," Mrs. Lambchop said. She lowered him between the bars

and moved him carefully up and down and from side to side, so that he could search the whole floor of the shaft.

Two **policemen** came by and **stare**d at Mrs. Lambchop as she stood holding the long lace that ran down through the grating. She pretended not to **notice** them.

"What's the matter, lady?" the first policeman asked. "Is your yo-yo⋆ **stuck**?"

"I am not playing with a yo-yo!" Mrs. Lambchop said **sharp**ly. "My son is at the other end of this lace, if you must know."

"Get the **net**,⋇ Harry," said the second policeman. "We have caught a **cuckoo**!"

⋆ **yo-yo** 요요. 동그란 원형 두 개의 중심축을 연결하여 고정하고 그 축에 끈을 달아 늘어뜨리면 스스로 내려갔다 제자리로 돌아오는 장난감.

⋇ **get the net** 그물을 가져와서 그녀를 잡아 정신병원으로 보내라는 의미이다.

Just then, down in the shaft, Stanley cried out, "**Hooray**!"

Mrs. Lambchop pulled him up and saw that he had the ring.

"Good for you, Stanley," she said. Then she turned angrily to the policemen.

"A cuckoo, indeed!" she said. "**Shame**!"

The policemen **apologize**d. "We didn't **get it**, lady," they said. "We have been **hasty**. We see that now."

"People should **think twice** before making **rude remark**s," said Mrs. Lambchop. "And then not make them at all."

The policemen **realize**d that was a good **rule** and said they would try to remember it.

One day Stanley got a letter from his friend Thomas Anthony Jeffrey, whose family had moved recently to California. A school vacation was about to begin, and Stanley was invited to spend it with the Jeffreys.

"Oh, boy!*" Stanley said. "I would love to go!"

Mr. Lambchop **sigh**ed. "A **round-trip** train or airplane ticket to California is very expensive," he said. "I will have to think of some cheaper way."

When Mr. Lambchop came home from the office that evening, he brought with him an **enormous** brown-paper **envelope**.

★ **boy** 여기에서는 '소년'이라는 뜻이 아니라, '맙소사!' 또는 '어머나!'라는 의미의 놀람·기쁨·아픔 등을 나타내는 표현으로 쓰였다.

"Now then, Stanley," he said. "Try this for size."

The envelope **fit** Stanley very well. There

was even **room left over**, Mrs. Lambchop **discover**ed, for an egg-salad sandwich made with thin bread, and a **toothbrush case** filled with milk.

They had to put a great many **stamp**s on the envelope to pay for both **airmail** and **insurance**, but it was still much less expensive than a train or airplane ticket to California.

The next day Mr. and Mrs. Lambchop slid Stanley into his envelope, along with the egg-salad sandwich and the toothbrush case full of milk, and mailed him from the box* on the corner. The envelope had to be **fold**ed to fit through

---

★ **box** 여기에서는 '우체통(postbox)'을 가리킨다.

26

the **slot**, but Stanley was a **limber** boy, and inside the box he **straighten**ed right up again.

Mrs. Lambchop was nervous because Stanley had never been away from home alone before. She **rap**ped on the box.

"Can you hear me, **dear**?" she called. "Are you all right?"

Stanley's voice came quite clearly. "I'm fine. Can I eat my sandwich now?"

"Wait an hour. And try not to get **overheated**, dear," Mrs. Lambchop said. Then she and Mr. Lambchop cried out, "Good-bye, good-bye!" and went home.

Stanley had a fine time in California. When the visit was over, the Jeffreys returned him in a beautiful white envelope they had made themselves. It had red-and-blue **markings** to show that it was airmail, and Thomas Jeffrey had lettered it **"Valuable"** and **"Fragile"** and "This End Up" on both sides.

Back home Stanley told his family that he had been **handled** so carefully he never felt a single **bump**. Mr. Lambchop said it **proved** that **jet** planes were wonderful, and so was the Postal Service, and that this was a great age in which to live.

Stanley thought so too.

Stanley the Kite

Mr. Lambchop had always liked to take the boys out with him on Sunday afternoons, to a museum or roller-skating in the park, but it was difficult when they were crossing streets or moving about in crowds. Stanley and Arthur would often be **jostle**d from his side and Mr. Lambchop worried about **speed**ing taxis or

that hurrying people might **accidenta**lly **knock** them down.

It was easier after Stanley got flat.

Mr. Lambchop **discover**ed that he could **roll** Stanley up without hurting him at all. He would **tie** a piece of **string** around Stanley to keep him from unrolling and make a little **loop** in the string for himself. It was as simple as carrying a **parcel**, and he could hold on to Arthur with the other hand.

Stanley did not mind being carried because he had never much liked to walk. Arthur didn't like to walk either, but he had to. It made him mad.

One Sunday afternoon, in the street, they met Ralph Jones, an old **college** friend of Mr. Lambchop's.

"Well, George, I see you have bought some **wallpaper**," Mr. Jones said. "Going to **decorate** your house, I suppose?"

"Wallpaper?" said Mr. Lambchop. "Oh, no. This is my son Stanley."

He **undid** the string and Stanley unrolled.

"How do you do?" Stanley said.

"Nice to meet you, young **feller**," said Mr. Jones. "George," he said to Mr. Lambchop, "that boy is flat."

"Smart, too," Mr. Lambchop said. "Stanley is third from the top in his class at school."

"**Phooey**!" said Arthur.

"This is my younger son, Arthur," Mr. Lambchop said. "And he will **apologize** for his **rude**ness."

Arthur could only **blush** and apologize.

Mr. Lambchop rolled Stanley up again
and they **set out** for home. It rained quite
hard while they were on the way. Stanley,
of course, **hardly** got wet at all, just around
the **edge**s, but Arthur got **soak**ed.

Late that night Mr. and Mrs. Lambchop
heard a noise out in the living room. They
found Arthur lying on the floor near the
bookcase. He had **pile**d a great many
volumes of the *Encyclopaedia Britannica*★ on
top of himself.

"Put some more on me," Arthur said
when he saw them. "Don't just stand there.
Help me."

★ **Encyclopaedia Britannica** 브리태니커 백과사전. 영어권에서 가장 오
래된 백과사전.

Mr. and Mrs. Lambchop sent him back to bed, but the next morning they spoke to Stanley. "Arthur can't help being **jealous**," they said. "Be nice to him. You're his big brother, **after all**."

The next Sunday, Stanley and Arthur went to the park by themselves. The day was sunny, but **windy** too, and many older boys were flying beautiful, **enormous** kites with long **tail**s, made in all the colors of the rainbow.

Arthur **sigh**ed. "**Someday**," he said, "I will have a big kite, and I will win a kite-flying **contest** and be famous like everyone else. *Nobody* knows who I am these days."

Stanley remembered what his parents

had said. He went to a boy whose kite was broken and borrowed a large **spool** of string.

"You can fly me, Arthur," he said. "Come on."

He **attach**ed the string to himself and gave Arthur the spool to hold. He ran lightly across the grass, **sideways** to **get up** speed, and then he turned to meet the **breeze**.

Up, up, up . . . UP! went Stanley, being a kite.

He knew just how to manage on the **gust**s of wind. He faced full into the wind if he wanted to rise, and let it take him from behind when he wanted speed.

He had only to turn his thin edge to the wind, carefully, a little at a time, so that it did not hold him, and then he would **slip graceful**ly down toward the earth again.

Arthur let out all the string, and Stanley **soar**ed high above the trees, a beautiful **sight** in his red shirt and blue **trousers** against the **pale** blue sky.

Everyone in the park stood **still** to watch.

Stanley **swoop**ed right and then left in long, **match**ed swoops. He held his arms by his sides and **zoom**ed at the ground like a rocket and **curve**d up again toward the sun. He side-slipped★ and **circle**d, and made **figure** eights and crosses and a star.

Nobody has ever flown the way Stanley Lambchop flew that day. Probably no one ever will again.

After a while, of course, people grew **tired** of watching, and Arthur got tired of running about with the empty spool.

★ **side-slip** 횡전(橫轉). 항공기가 수평 비행 도중에 옆으로 한 번 회전하고 다시 수평 비행을 계속하는 특수 비행.

Stanley **went** right **on**, though, **show**ing **off**.

Three boys came up to Arthur and invited him to join them for a hot dog and some soda pop.* Arthur left the spool **wedge**d in the **fork** of a tree. He did not **notice**, while he was eating the hot dog, that the wind was blowing the string and **tangling** it about the tree.

The string got shorter and shorter, but Stanley did not **realize** how low he was until leaves **brush**ed his feet, and then it was too late.

★ **soda pop** 탄산음료. 이산화탄소를 물에 녹여 만든 시원한 음료.

He got **stuck** in the **branch**es. Fifteen
minutes passed before Arthur and the
other boys heard his cries and climbed up
to set him free.

Stanley would not speak to his brother
that evening, and at **bedtime**, even though
Arthur had apologized, he was still **cross**.

Alone with Mr. Lambchop in the living
room, Mrs. Lambchop sighed and shook
her head. "You're at the office all day,
having fun," she said. "You don't realize
what I **go through** with the boys. They're
very difficult."

"Kids are like that," Mr. Lambchop said.
"**Phase**s. Be **patient, dear.**"

The Museum Thieves

Mr. and Mrs. O. Jay Dart lived in the apartment above the Lambchops. Mr. Dart was an important man, the **director** of the Famous Museum of Art **downtown** in the city.

Stanley Lambchop had **notice**d in the elevator that Mr. Dart, who was **ordinarily** a **cheerful** man, had become quite **gloomy**, but he had no idea what the reason was.

And then at breakfast one morning he heard Mr. and Mrs. Lambchop talking about Mr. Dart.

"I see," said Mr. Lambchop, reading the paper over his coffee cup, "that still another painting has been **stolen** from the Famous Museum. It says here that Mr. O. Jay Dart, the director, is at his **wits**' end."

"Oh, **dear**! Are the police no help?" Mrs. Lambchop asked.

"It seems not," said Mr. Lambchop. "Listen to what the **Chief** of Police told the newspaper. 'We **suspect** a **gang** of **sneak** thieves. These are the worst kind. They work by sneakery,* which makes them

---

★ **sneakery** 작가가 만든 단어로 '은밀한 행동' 또는 '좀도둑질'이라는 뜻으로 해석할 수 있다.

very difficult to catch. However, my men and I will keep trying. **Meanwhile**, I hope people will buy tickets for the **Policemen**'s **Ball** and not park their cars where **sign**s

say don't.'"

The next morning Stanley Lambchop heard Mr. Dart talking to his wife in the elevator.

"These sneak thieves work at night," Mr. Dart said. "It is very hard for our **guard**s to stay awake when they have been on **duty** all day. And the Famous Museum is so big, we cannot guard every picture at the same time. I fear it is **hopeless**, hopeless, hopeless!"

Suddenly, as if an **electric** light **bulb** had lit up in the air above his head, **giving out** little shooting lines of excitement, Stanley Lambchop had an idea. He told it to Mr. Dart.

"Stanley," Mr. Dart said, "if your mother will give her **permission**, I will **put** you and your plan **to work** this very night!"

Mrs. Lambchop gave her permission. "But you will have to take a long **nap** this afternoon," she said. "I won't have you up till all hours unless you do."

That evening, after a long nap, Stanley went with Mr. Dart to the Famous Museum. Mr. Dart took him into the main hall, where the biggest and most important paintings were hung. He pointed to a huge painting that showed a **beard**ed man, wearing a **floppy** velvet* hat, playing a violin for a lady who lay on a **couch**. There

---

★ velvet 벨벳. 짧고 부드러운 솜털이 있는 원단.

52

was a half-man, half-horse person standing behind them, and three fat children with wings were flying around above. That, Mr. Dart explained, was the most expensive painting in the world!

There was an empty picture **frame** on the **opposite** wall. We shall hear more about that later on.

Mr. Dart took Stanley into his office and said, "It is time for you to put on a **disguise**."

"I already thought of that," Stanley Lambchop said, "and I brought one. My cowboy **suit**. It has a red bandanna⋆ that I can **tie** over my face. Nobody will

---

⋆ **bandanna** 반다나. 목이나 머리에 두르는 화려한 색상의 스카프.

recognize me in a million years."

"No," Mr. Dart said. "You will have to wear the disguise I have chosen."

From a **closet** he took a white dress with a blue **sash**, a pair of shiny little **pointed** shoes, a wide **straw** hat with a blue band that **match**ed the sash, and a **wig** and a **stick**. The wig was made of **blond** hair, and done in **ringlet**s. The stick was **curve**d at the top and it, too, had a blue ribbon on it.

"In this **shepherdess** disguise," Mr. Dart said, "you will look like a painting that **belong**s in the main hall. We do not have cowboy pictures in the main hall."

Stanley was so **disgust**ed, he could **hardly** speak. "I will look like a girl, that's what I will look like," he said. "I wish I

had never had my idea."

But he was a good **sport**, so he put on the disguise.

Back in the main hall, Mr. Dart helped Stanley climb up into the empty picture frame. Stanley was able to stay in place because Mr. Dart had **clever**ly put four small **spike**s in the wall, one for each hand and foot.

The frame was a perfect **fit**. Against the wall, Stanley looked just like a picture.

"**Except** for one thing," Mr. Dart said. "Shepherdesses are supposed to look happy. They smile at their sheep and at the sky. You look **fierce**, not happy, Stanley."

Stanley tried hard to get a **faraway** look in his eyes and even to smile a little bit.

Mr. Dart stood back a few feet and **stare**d at him for a moment. "Well," he said, "it may not be art, but I know what I like."

He went off to make sure that certain other parts of Stanley's plan were **take**n **care of**, and Stanley was left alone.

It was very dark in the main hall. A little bit of moonlight came through the windows, and Stanley could just **make out** the world's most expensive painting on the opposite wall. He felt as though the bearded man with the violin and the lady on the couch and the half-horse person and the **winged** children were all waiting, as he was, for something to happen.

Time passed and he got **tired**er and

tireder. Anyone would be tired this late at night, especially if he had to stand in a picture frame balancing on little spikes.

Maybe they won't come, Stanley thought. Maybe the sneak thieves won't come at all.

The moon went behind a cloud and then the main hall was **pitch-dark**. It seemed to get quieter, too, with the darkness. There was **absolute**ly no sound at all. Stanley felt the hair on the back of his neck **prickle beneath** the golden **curl**s of the wig.

Cr-eee-eee-k . . .

The **creak**ing sound came from right out in the middle of the main hall, and even as he heard it, Stanley saw, in the same place, a **tiny** yellow **glow** of light!

The creaking came again, and the glow got bigger. A **trapdoor** had opened in the floor, and two men came up through it into the hall!

Stanley understood everything **all at once**. These must be the sneak thieves! They had a secret trapdoor **entrance** into the museum from outside. That was why they had never been caught. And now, tonight, they were back to steal the most expensive painting in the world!

He held very **still** in his picture frame and listened to the sneak thieves.

"This is it, Max," said the first one. "This

is where we art **rob**bers **pull a sensational job whilst** the **civilized community** sleeps."

"Right, Luther," said the other man. "In all this great city, there is no one to suspect us."

Ha, ha! thought Stanley Lambchop. That's what you think!

The sneak thieves put down their **lantern** and took the world's most expensive painting off the wall.

"What would we do to anyone who tried to **capture** us, Max?" the first man asked.

"We would kill him. What else?" his

friend replied.

That was enough to **frighten** Stanley, and he was even more frightened when Luther came over and stared at him.

"This sheep girl," Luther said. "I thought

sheep girls were supposed to smile, Max. This one looks **scare**d."

Just **in time**, Stanley managed to get a faraway look in his eyes again and to smile, sort of.

"You're crazy, Luther," Max said. "She's smiling. And what a pretty little thing she is, too."

That made Stanley **furious**. He waited until the sneak thieves had turned back to the world's most expensive painting, and he shouted in his loudest, most **terrify**ing voice: "POLICE! POLICE! MR. DART! THE SNEAK THIEVES ARE HERE!"

The sneak thieves looked at each other. "Max," said the first one, very quietly. "I think I heard the sheep girl **yell**."

"I think I did too," said Max in a **quiver**y voice. "Oh, boy! Yelling pictures. We both need a **rest**."

"You'll get a rest, all right!" shouted Mr. Dart, **rush**ing in with the Chief of Police

and lots of guards and policemen behind him. "You'll get *ar-rested*, that's what! Ha, ha, ha!"

The sneak thieves **were** too **mixed up** by Mr. Dart's **joke** and too frightened by the policemen to **put up** a fight.

Before they knew it, they had been **handcuff**ed and led away to **jail**.

The next morning in the office of the Chief of Police, Stanley Lambchop got a medal. The day after that his picture was in all the newspapers.

Arthur's Good Idea

For a while Stanley Lambchop was a
famous name. Everywhere that Stanley
went, people **stare**d and pointed at him.
He could hear them **whisper**, "Over there,
Agnes, over there! That must be Stanley
Lambchop, the one who caught the **sneak**
thieves . . ." and things like that.

But after a few weeks the whispering

and the staring stopped. People had other things to think about. Stanley did not mind. Being famous had been fun, but enough was enough.

And then came a further change, and it was not a **pleasant** one. People began to laugh and **make fun of** him as he passed by. "Hello, Super-**Skinny**!" they would shout, and even **rude**r things, about the way he looked.

Stanley told his parents how he felt. "It's the other kids I mostly mind," he said. "They don't like me anymore because I'm different. Flat."

"**Shame** on them," Mrs. Lambchop said. "It is wrong to dislike people for their shapes. Or their **religion, for that matter,** or the color of their skin."

"I know," Stanley said. "Only maybe it's impossible for everybody to like *everybody*."

"Perhaps," said Mrs. Lambchop. "But they can try."

Later that night Arthur Lambchop was woken by the sound of crying. In the darkness he **crept** across the room and **knelt** by Stanley's bed.

"Are you okay?" he said.

"Go away," Stanley said.

"Don't be mad at me," Arthur said. "You're still mad because I let you get **tangle**d the day you were my **kite**, I guess."

"**Skip it**, will you?" Stanley said. "I'm

not mad. Go away."

"Please let's be friends. . . ." Arthur couldn't help crying a little, too. "Oh, Stanley," he said. "Please tell me what's wrong."

Stanley waited for a long time before he spoke. "The thing is," he said, "I'm just not happy anymore. I'm **tired** of being flat. I want to be a **regular** shape again, like other people. But I'll have to **go on** being flat forever. It makes me sick."

"Oh, Stanley," Arthur said. He dried his tears on a corner of Stanley's **sheet** and could think of nothing more to say.

"Don't talk about what I just said," Stanley told him. "I don't want the **folk**s to worry. That would only make it worse."

"You're brave," Arthur said. "You really are."

He took hold of Stanley's hand. The two brothers sat together in the darkness, being friends. They were both sad, but each one felt a *little* better than he had before.

Then, suddenly, though he was not even trying to think, Arthur had an idea. He jumped up and turned on the light and ran to the big **storage** box where toys and things were kept. He began to **rummage** in the box.

Stanley sat up in bed to watch.

Arthur **flung** aside a football and some lead soldiers* and airplane models and lots of wooden blocks,* and then he said,

"Aha!" He had found what he wanted—
an old bicycle **pump**. He held it up, and
Stanley and he looked at each other.

"Okay," Stanley said at last. "But **take
it easy**." He put the end of the long pump
hose in his mouth and **clamp**ed his lips
tightly about it so that no air could escape.

"I'll go slowly," Arthur said. "If it hurts
or anything, **wiggle** your hand at me."

Then he began to pump. At first
nothing happened **except** that Stanley's
cheeks **bulge**d a bit. Arthur watched his
hand, but there was no wiggle **signal**, so
he pumped on. Then, suddenly, Stanley's

★ **lead soldier** 주석 등의 쇠로 만든 장난감 병정.
✳ **block** 블록. 나무나 플라스틱으로 만들어진 작은 토막을 조립하여 건물이
나 로봇 등을 만드는 장난감.

top half began to **swell**.

"It's working! It's working!" shouted Arthur, pumping away.

Stanley **spread** his arms so that the air could get around inside him more easily. He got bigger and bigger. The buttons of his **pajama** top **burst** off—*Pop! Pop! Pop!* A moment more and he was all **round**ed out; head and body, arms and legs. But not his right foot. That stayed flat.

Arthur stopped pumping. "It's like trying to do the very last bit of those long balloons," he said. "Maybe a shake would help."

Stanley shook his right foot twice, and with a little *whooshing* sound it swelled out to **match** the left one. There stood

Stanley Lambchop as he **used to** be, as if he had never been flat at all.

"Thank you, Arthur," Stanley said. "Thank you very much."

The brothers were shaking hands when Mr. Lambchop **strode** into the room with Mrs. Lambchop right behind him. "We heard you!" said Mr. Lambchop. "Up and talking when you ought to be asleep, eh? Shame on—"

"GEORGE!" said Mrs. Lambchop. "Stanley's *round* again!"

"You're right!" said Mr. Lambchop, **noticing**. "Good for you, Stanley!"

"I'm the one who did it," Arthur said. "I blew him up."

Everyone was **terribly** excited and

happy, of course. Mrs. Lambchop made
hot chocolate to **celebrate** the **occasion**,
and several **toast**s were drunk to Arthur
for his **clever**ness.

When the little party was over, Mr. and Mrs. Lambchop **tuck**ed the boys back into their beds and kissed them, and then they turned out the light. "Good night," they said.

"Good night," said Stanley and Arthur.

It had been a long and **tiring** day. Very soon all the Lambchops were asleep.

The End

스탠리의 첫 번째 모험!

스탠리의 첫 번째 모험!

CONTENTS

미국 초등학생 사이에서 저스틴 비버보다 더 유명한 소년, 플랫 스탠리!

『플랫 스탠리(Flat Stanley)』 시리즈는 미국의 작가 제프 브라운(Jeff Brown)이 쓴 책으로, 한밤중에 몸 위로 떨어진 거대한 게시판에 눌려 납작해진(flat) 스탠리 가 겪는 다양한 모험을 담고 있습니다. 플랫 스탠리는 아동 도서이지만 부모님 들과 선생님들에게도 큰 사랑을 받으며, 출간된 지 50년이 넘은 지금까지 여러 세대를 아우르며 독자들에게 재미를 주고 있습니다. 미국에서만 100만 부 이상 판매된 『플랫 스탠리』 시리즈는 기존 챕터북 시리즈와 함께 플랫 스탠리의 세계 모험(Flat Stanley's Worldwide Adventures) 시리즈, 리더스북 등 다양한 형태로 출판되었고, 여러 언어로 번역되어 전 세계 독자들의 마음을 사로잡았습니다. 주인공 스탠리가 그려진 종이 인형을 만들어 이를 우편으로 원하는 사람에게 보 내는 플랫 스탠리 프로젝트(The Flat Stanley Project)가 1995년에 시작된 이후, 이 책은 더 많은 관심을 받게 되었습니다. 유명 연예인은 물론 오바마 대통령까 지 이 종이 인형과 함께 사진을 찍어 공유하는 등, 수많은 사례를 통해 시리즈의 높은 인기를 짐작할 수 있습니다.

이러한 『플랫 스탠리』 시리즈는 한국에서도 널리 알려져 '엄마표·아빠표 영어' 를 진행하는 부모님과 초보 영어 학습자라면 반드시 읽어야 하는 영어원서로 자 리 잡았습니다. 렉사일 지수가 최대 640L인 플랫 스탠리는 간결하지만 필수적 인 어휘로 쓰여, 영어원서가 친숙하지 않은 학습자들에게도 즐거운 원서 읽기 경험을 선사할 것입니다.

번역과 단어장이 포함된 워크북, 그리고 오디오북까지 담긴 풀 패키지!

이 책은 영어원서 『플랫 스탠리』 시리즈에, 탁월한 학습 효과를 거둘 수 있도록 다양한 콘텐츠를 덧붙인 책입니다.

- 영어원서: 본문에 나온 어려운 어휘에 볼드 처리가 되어 있어 단어를 더욱 분 명하게 인지할 수 있고, 문맥에 따른 자연스러운 암기 효과를 얻을 수 있습니다.
- 단어장: 원서에 볼드 처리된 어휘의 의미가 완벽하게 정리되어 있어 사전 없 이 원서를 수월하게 읽을 수 있으며, 반복해서 등장하는 단어에 '복습' 표기를 하여 자연스럽게 복습을 돕도록 구성했습니다.

- 번역: 영문과 비교할 수 있도록 직역에 가까운 번역을 담았습니다. 원서 읽기에 익숙하지 않은 초보 학습자도 어려움 없이 내용을 파악할 수 있습니다.
- 퀴즈: 챕터별로 내용을 확인하는 이해력 점검 퀴즈가 들어 있습니다.
- 오디오북: 미국 현지에서 판매 중인 빠른 속도의 오디오북(분당 약 145단어)과 국내에서 녹음된 따라 읽기용 오디오북(분당 약 110단어)을 기본으로 포함하고 있어, 듣기 훈련은 물론 소리 내어 읽기에까지 폭넓게 활용할 수 있습니다.

이 책의 수준과 타깃 독자
- 미국 원어민 기준: 유치원 ∼ 초등학교 저학년
- 한국 학습자 기준: 초등학교 저학년 ∼ 중학생
- 영어원서 완독 경험이 없는 초보 영어 학습자
- 도서 분량: 약 5,900단어
- 비슷한 수준의 다른 챕터북: Arthur Chapter Book,* The Zack Files,* Tales from the Odyssey,* Junie B. Jones,* Magic Tree House, Marvin Redpost

  ★「롱테일 에디션」으로 출간된 도서

『플랫 스탠리』 이렇게 읽어 보세요!

- **단어 암기는 이렇게!** 처음 리딩을 시작하기 전, 오늘 읽을 챕터에 나오는 단어들을 눈으로 쭉 훑어봅니다. 모르는 단어는 좀 더 주의 깊게 보되, 손으로 쓰면서 완벽하게 암기할 필요는 없습니다. 본문을 읽으면서 이 단어를 다시 만나게 되는데, 그 과정에서 단어의 쓰임새와 어감을 자연스럽게 익히게 됩니다. 이렇게 책을 읽은 후에 단어를 다시 한번 복습하세요. 복습할 때는 중요하다고 생각하는 단어들을 손으로 쓰면서 꼼꼼하게 외우는 것도 좋습니다. 이런 방식으로 책을 읽으면 많은 단어를 빠르고 부담 없이 익힐 수 있습니다.

- **리딩할 때는 리딩에만 집중하자!** 원서를 읽는 중간중간 모르는 단어가 나온다고 워크북을 바로 펼쳐 보거나, 곧바로 번역을 찾아보는 것은 크게 도움이 되지 않습니다. 모르는 단어나 이해되지 않는 문장들은 따로 가볍게 표시만 해 두고, 전체적인 맥락을 파악하며 속도감 있게 읽어 나가세요. 리딩을 할 때는 속

도에 대한 긴장감을 잃지 않으면서 리딩에만 집중하는 것이 좋습니다. 모르는 단어와 문장은 리딩을 마친 후에 한꺼번에 정리하는 '리뷰' 시간을 통해 점검하는 시간을 가지면 됩니다. 리뷰를 할 때는 번역은 물론 단어장과 사전도 꼼꼼하게 확인하면서 어떤 이유에서 이해가 되지 않았는지 생각해 봅니다.

● **번역 활용은 이렇게!** 이해가 가지 않는 문장은 번역을 통해서 그 의미를 파악할 수 있습니다. 하지만 한국어와 영어는 정확히 1:1 대응이 되지 않기 때문에 번역을 활용하는 데에도 지혜가 필요합니다. 의역이 된 부분까지 억지로 의미를 대응해서 이해하려고 하기보다, 어떻게 그런 의미가 만들어진 것인지 추측하면서 번역은 참고 자료로 활용하는 것이 좋습니다.

● **듣기 훈련은 이렇게!** 리스닝 실력을 향상시키고 싶다면 오디오북을 적극적으로 활용해 보세요. 처음에는 오디오북을 틀어 놓고 눈으로 해당 내용을 따라 읽으면서 훈련을 하고, 이것이 익숙해지면 오디오북만 틀어 놓고 '귀를 통해' 책을 읽어 보세요. 눈으로 읽지 않은 책이라도 귀를 통해 이해할 수 있을 정도가 되면, 이후에 영어 듣기로 어려움을 겪는 일은 거의 없을 것입니다.

● **소리 내어 읽고 녹음하자!** 이 책은 특히 소리 내어 읽기(voice reading)에 최적화된 문장 길이와 구조를 가지고 있습니다. 오디오북 기본 구성에 포함된 '따라 읽기용' 오디오북을 활용해 소리 내어 읽기 훈련을 시작해 보세요! 내가 읽은 것을 녹음하고 들어보는 과정을 통해 자연스럽게 어휘와 표현을 복습하고, 의식적·무의식적으로 발음을 교정하게 됩니다. 이렇게 영어로 소리를 만들어 본 경험은 이후 탄탄한 스피킹 실력의 밑거름이 될 것입니다.

● **2~3번 반복해서 읽자!** 영어 초보자라면 처음부터 완벽하게 이해하려고 하는 것보다는 2~3회 반복해서 읽을 것을 추천합니다. 처음 원서를 읽을 때는 생소한 단어들과 스토리 때문에 내용 파악에 급급할 수밖에 없습니다. 하지만 일단 내용을 파악한 후에 다시 읽으면 문장 구조나 어휘의 활용에 더 집중하게 되고, 원서를 더 깊이 있게 읽을 수 있습니다. 그 과정에서 리딩 속도에 탄력이 붙고 리딩 실력 또한 더 확고히 다지게 됩니다.

• **'시리즈'로 꾸준히 읽자!** 한 작가의 책을 시리즈로 읽는 것 또한 영어 실력 향상에 큰 도움이 됩니다. 같은 등장인물이 다시 나오기 때문에 내용 파악이 더 수월할 뿐 아니라, 작가가 사용하는 어휘와 표현들도 반복되기 때문에 탁월한 복습 효과까지 얻을 수 있습니다. 롱테일북스의 『플랫 스탠리』 시리즈는 현재 6권, 총 35,700단어 분량이 출간되어 있습니다. 시리즈를 꾸준히 읽다 보면 영어 실력이 자연스럽게 향상될 것입니다.

원서 본문 구성

내용이 담긴 원서 본문입니다.
원어민이 읽는 일반 원서와 같은 텍스트지만, 암기해야 할 중요 어휘들은 볼드체로 표시되어 있습니다. 이 어휘들은 지금 들고 계신 워크북에 챕터별로 정리되어 있습니다.

학습 심리학 연구 결과에 따르면, 한 단어씩 따로 외우는 단어 암기는 거의 효과가 없다고 합니다. 단어를 제대로 외우기 위해서는 문맥(context) 속에서 단어를 암기해야 하며, 한 단어당 문맥 속에서 15번 이상 마주칠 때 완벽하게 암기할 수 있다고 합니다. 이 책의 본문에서는 중요 어휘를 볼드체로 강조하여, 문맥 속의 단어들을 더 확실히 인지(word cognition in context)하도록 돕고 있습니다. 또한 대부분의 중요 단어들은 다른 챕터에서도 반복해서 등장하기 때문에 이 책을 읽는 것만으로도 자연스럽게 어휘력을 향상시킬 수 있습니다.

본문 하단에는 내용 이해를 돕기 위한 '각주'가 첨가되어 있습니다. 각주는 굳이 암기할 필요는 없지만, 알아 두면 도움이 될 만한 정보를 설명하고 있습니다. 각주를 참고하면 스토리를 더 깊이 있게 이해할 수 있어 원서를 읽는 재미가 배가됩니다.

워크북(Workbook) 구성

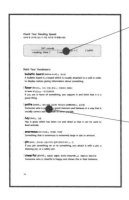

Check Your Reading Speed
해당 챕터의 단어 수가 기록되어 있어, 리딩 속도를 측정할 수 있습니다. 특히 리딩 속도를 중시하는 독자들이 유용하게 사용할 수 있습니다.

Build Your Vocabulary
본문에 볼드 표시되어 있는 단어들이 정리되어 있습니다. 리딩 전·후에 반복해서 보면 원서를 더욱 쉽게 읽을 수 있고, 어휘력도 빠르게 향상될 것입니다.

단어는 〈스펠링 – 빈도 – 발음기호 – 품사 – 한글 뜻 – 영문 뜻〉 순서로 표기되어 있으며 빈도 표시(★)가 많을수록 필수 어휘입니다. 반복해서 등장하는 단어는 빈도 대신 '복습'으로 표기되어 있습니다. 품사는 아래와 같이 표기했습니다.

n. 명사 | a. 형용사 | ad. 부사 | v. 동사
conj. 접속사 | prep. 전치사 | int. 감탄사 | idiom 숙어 및 관용구

Comprehension Quiz
간단한 퀴즈를 통해 읽은 내용에 대한 이해력을 점검해 볼 수 있습니다.

한국어 번역
영문과 비교할 수 있도록 최대한 직역에 가까운 번역을 담았습니다.

오디오북 구성

이 책에는 '듣기 훈련'과 '소리 내어 읽기 훈련'을 위한 2가지 종류의 오디오북이 기본으로 포함되어 있습니다.

- 듣기 훈련용 오디오북: 분당 145단어 속도 (미국 현지에서 판매 중인 오디오북)
- 따라 읽기용 오디오북: 분당 110단어 속도 (소리 내어 읽기 훈련용 오디오북)

 QR 코드를 인식하여 따라 읽기용 & 듣기 훈련용 두 가지 오디오북을 들어보세요! 더불어 롱테일북스 홈페이지 (www.longtailbooks.co.kr)에서도 오디오북 MP3 파일을 다운로드 받을 수 있습니다.

The Big Bulletin Board

1. **Why did Mr. Lambchop tell Arthur that hay was for horses?**

   A. He wanted to teach Arthur about horses.

   B. He wanted Arthur to get out of bed.

   C. He wanted Arthur to use more polite language.

   D. He wanted Arthur to eat a proper breakfast.

2. **Why had Mr. Lambchop given Stanley and Arthur a bulletin board?**

   A. So that they could display photos and messages on it.

   B. So that they could focus better on their homework.

   C. So that they could make their room more organized.

   D. So that they could stop pinning pictures on the wall.

3. What happened to the bulletin board last night?

    A. It fell and woke up Arthur.

    B. It fell and made Mr. and Mrs. Lambchop shout.

    C. It fell on the floor and broke.

    D. It fell on top of Stanley.

4. What did Mrs. Lambchop and Stanley do after breakfast?

    A. They took Arthur to school.

    B. They put the bulletin board back on the wall.

    C. They visited the doctor's office.

    D. They went to a clothing shop.

5. Why were Stanley's measurements taken?

    A. Dr. Dan was worried that Stanley had gotten shorter.

    B. The nurse was curious about how thick Stanley was.

    C. Mrs. Lambchop thought that Stanley's clothes would have to be altered.

    D. Stanley wanted to know what size shirt and pants he should buy.

Check Your Reading Speed

1분에 몇 단어를 읽는지 리딩 속도를 측정해보세요.

$$\frac{347 \ words}{reading \ time \ (\qquad) \ sec} \times 60 = (\qquad) \ WPM$$

Build Your Vocabulary

bulletin board [búlitən bɔːrd] n. 게시판
A bulletin board is a board which is usually attached to a wall in order to display notices giving information about something.

favor [féivər] n. 지지, 인정; 호의; v. 선호하다; 알맞다
(in favor of idiom ~에 찬성하여)
If you are in favor of something, you support it and think that it is a good thing.

polite [pəláit] a. 예의 바른, 공손한; 예의상의 (politeness n. 공손함)
Someone who is polite has good manners and behaves in a way that is socially correct and not rude to other people.

hay [hei] n. 건초
Hay is grass which has been cut and dried so that it can be used to feed animals.

enormous [inɔ́ːrməs] a. 막대한, 거대한
Something that is enormous is extremely large in size or amount.

pin [pin] v. (핀으로) 고정시키다; 꼼짝 못하게 하다; n. 핀
If you pin something on or to something, you attach it with a pin, a drawing pin, or a safety pin.

cheerful [ʧíərfəl] a. 발랄한, 쾌활한; 쾌적한 (cheerfully ad. 쾌활하게, 명랑하게)
Someone who is cheerful is happy and shows this in their behavior.

beneath [biníːθ] prep. 아래에
Something that is beneath another thing is under the other thing.

heavens [hévəns] int. 맙소사!
You say 'heavens!' or 'good heavens!' to express surprise or to emphasize that you agree or disagree with someone.

gosh [gaʃ] int. (놀람·기쁨을 나타내어) 어머!, 뭐라고!
Some people say 'gosh' when they are surprised.

examine [igzǽmin] v. 진찰하다; 조사하다; 시험을 실시하다 (examination n. 진찰)
If a doctor examines you, he or she looks at your body, feels it, or does simple tests in order to check how healthy you are.

tickle [tikl] n. 간지러움; (장난으로) 간지럽히기; v. 간질간질하다; 간지럽히다
(tickly a. (= ticklish) 간질간질한; 간지럼을 잘 타는)
Someone who is ticklish is sensitive to being tickled, and laughs as soon as you tickle them.

case [keis] n. (특정한 상황의) 경우; 사건; 용기, 통, 상자
A case is a person or their particular problem that a doctor, social worker, or other professional is dealing with.

keep an eye on idiom ~을 계속 지켜보다
If you keep an eye on someone or something, you watch or check them to make sure that they are safe.

fellow [félou] n. 녀석, 친구; 동료; a. 동료의
A fellow is a man or boy.

marvel [máːrvəl] v. 경이로워하다, 경탄하다; n. 경이(로운 사람·것)
If you marvel at something, you express your great surprise, wonder, or admiration.

alter [ɔ́ːltər] v. (옷을) 고치다; 변하다, 달라지다
If something alters or if you alter it, it changes.

tailor [téilər] n. 재단사; v. 맞추다, 조정하다
A tailor is a person whose job is to make men's clothes.

* **measure** [méʒər] v. 측정하다; 판단하다; n. 조치, 정책; 척도
(measurement n. (pl.) 치수; 측정)

Your measurements are the size of your waist, chest, hips, and other parts of your body, which you need to know when you are buying clothes.

Being Flat

1. **What was one thing Stanley could enjoy doing because he was flat?**

    A. He could slide under closed doors.

    B. He could avoid taking baths.

    C. He could climb up to high places.

    D. He could skip school.

2. **Why did Mrs. Lambchop lower Stanley between the bars of a grating?**

    A. So that Stanley would stop crying.

    B. So that Stanley could look for his shoelaces.

    C. So that Stanley could hide from the police.

    D. So that Stanley could find her ring.

3. What did the policemen think of Mrs. Lambchop at first?
    A. They thought she was having a good time.
    B. They thought she was going to steal something.
    C. They thought she was acting weird.
    D. They thought she was in danger.

4. Why did Mr. Lambchop decide to send Stanley to California in an envelope?
    A. It was faster than going by train or airplane.
    B. It was cheaper than buying a train or airplane ticket.
    C. It was safer than taking a train or airplane.
    D. It was more exciting than traveling by train or airplane.

5. What did Stanley say about his experience traveling by airmail?
    A. It was a boring journey.
    B. It was a scary journey.
    C. It was a long journey.
    D. It was a smooth journey.

Check Your Reading Speed

1분에 몇 단어를 읽는지 리딩 속도를 측정해보세요.

$$\frac{776 \text{ words}}{\text{reading time (} \quad \text{) sec}} \times 60 = (\quad) \text{ WPM}$$

Build Your Vocabulary

get used to idiom ~에 익숙해지다
If you get used to something or someone, you become familiar with it
or get to know them, so that you no longer feel that the thing or person
is unusual or surprising.

* **slide** [slaid] v. 미끄러지듯이 움직이다; 미끄러지다; 슬며시 넣다; n. 떨어짐; 미끄러짐
If you slide somewhere, you move there smoothly and quietly.

‡ **crack** [kræk] n. (좁은) 틈; (갈라져 생긴) 금; v. 갈라지다, 금이 가다; 깨지다, 부서지다
A crack is a very narrow gap between two things, or between two parts
of a thing.

‡ **silly** [síli] a. 우스꽝스러운; 어리석은, 바보 같은; n. 바보
If you say that someone or something is silly, you mean that they are
foolish, childish, or ridiculous.

‡ **jealous** [dʒéləs] a. 질투하는; 시샘하는
If you are jealous of another person's possessions or qualities, you feel
angry or bitter because you do not have them.

* **bang** [bæŋ] v. 쿵 하고 찧다; 쾅 하고 치다; 쾅 하고 닫다; n. 쾅 (하는 소리)
If you bang a part of your body, you accidentally knock it against
something and hurt yourself.

‡ **helpful** [hélpfəl] a. 도움이 되는
Something that is helpful makes a situation more pleasant or easier to
tolerate.

20

‡ **roll** [roul] v. 구르다, 굴러가다; (둥글게) 말다; n. 구르기; 굴리기
When something rolls or when you roll it, it moves along a surface, turning over many times.

⁎ **sidewalk** [sáidwɔːk] n. 보도, 인도
A sidewalk is a path with a hard surface by the side of a road.

‡ **bar** [baːr] n. (금속) 봉; 술집, 바; 카운터; 막대기 (모양의 것)
A bar is a long, straight, stiff piece of metal.

grating [gréitiŋ] n. (창문·하수구 등의) 쇠창살
A grating is a flat metal frame with rows of bars across it, which is fastened over a window or over a hole in a wall or the ground.

‡ **cover** [kʌ́vər] v. 덮다; 씌우다, 가리다; n. 몸을 숨길 곳; 덮개
If you cover something, you place something else over it in order to protect it, hide it, or close it.

⁎ **shaft** [ʃæft] n. (건물·지하의) 수직 통로, 수갱; 손잡이
A shaft is a long vertical passage, for example for an elevator.

⁎ **lace** [leis] n. (구두 등의) 끈, 엮은 끈; v. 끈으로 묶다; 가미하다, 첨가되다
Laces are thin pieces of material that are put through special holes in some types of clothing, especially shoes.

‡ **extra** [ékstrə] a. 여분의, 추가의; n. 추가되는 것; ad. 각별히, 특별히
You use extra to describe an amount, person, or thing that is added to others of the same kind, or that can be added to others of the same kind.

‡ **tie** [tai] v. (끈 등으로) 묶다; 결부시키다; n. 끈; (강한) 유대
If you tie two things together or tie them, you fasten them together with a knot.

‡ **lower** [lóuər] v. ~을 내리다; 낮추다
If you lower something, you move it slowly downward.

⁎ **policeman** [pəlíːsmən] n. (pl. policemen) 경찰관
A policeman is a person who is a member of the police force.

stare [stɛər] v. 빤히 쳐다보다, 응시하다; n. 빤히 쳐다보기, 응시
If you stare at someone or something, you look at them for a long time.

notice [nóutis] v. 알아채다, 인지하다; 주의하다; n. 신경씀, 주목, 알아챔
If you notice something or someone, you become aware of them.

stuck [stʌk] a. 움직일 수 없는, 꼼짝 못하는; 갇힌
If something is stuck in a particular position, it is fixed tightly in this position and is unable to move.

sharp [ʃɑːrp] a. (말이) 날카로운, 신랄한; (칼날 등이) 뾰족한, 예리한
(sharply ad. (비판 등을) 날카롭게, 신랄하게)
If someone says something in a sharp way, they say it suddenly and rather firmly or angrily, for example because they are warning or criticizing you.

net [net] n. 그물, 망; v. 그물로 잡다; (무엇을) 획득하다
A net is a piece of netting which is used for catching fish, insects, or animals.

cuckoo [kúːkuː] n. 미친 사람, 바보; [동물] 뻐꾸기; a. 미친
A cuckoo can refer to a foolish or crazy person.

hooray [huréi] int. 만세 (즐거움·찬성의 표시로 지르는 소리)
People sometimes shout 'Hooray!' when they are very happy and excited about something.

shame [ʃeim] n. 수치(심), 창피; 애석한 일; v. 창피스럽게 하다; 망신시키다
You can use shame in expressions such as shame on you and shame on him to indicate that someone ought to feel shame for something they have said or done.

apologize [əpálədʒàiz] v. 사과하다
When you apologize to someone, you say that you are sorry that you have hurt them or caused trouble for them.

get it idiom 이해하다; 야단맞다, 벌받다
To get it means to understand an argument or the person making it.

hasty [héisti] a. 성급한, 경솔한; 서두른
If you describe a person or their behavior as hasty, you mean that they are acting too quickly, without thinking carefully.

think twice idiom 신중히 생각하다
If you think twice about something, you carefully consider whether what you are planning to do is a good idea.

rude [ru:d] a. 무례한, 버릇없는; (나쁜 일이) 예상치 못한
When people are rude, they act in an impolite way toward other people or say impolite things about them.

remark [rimá:rk] n. 발언, 언급; 주목; v. 언급하다, 말하다
If you make a remark about something, you say something about it.

realize [rí:əlaiz] v. 깨닫다, 알아차리다; 실현하다, 달성하다
If you realize that something is true, you become aware of that fact or understand it.

rule [ru:l] n. 규칙; 통치, 지배; v. 통치하다, 다스리다, 지배하다
Rules are instructions that tell you what you are allowed to do and what you are not allowed to do.

sigh [sai] v. 한숨을 쉬다, 한숨짓다; 탄식하듯 말하다; n. 한숨
When you sigh, you let out a deep breath, as a way of expressing feelings such as disappointment, tiredness, or pleasure.

round-trip [raund-tríp] n. 왕복 여행
A round-trip ticket is a ticket for a train, bus, or plane that allows you to travel to a particular place and then back again.

enormous [inɔ́:rməs] a. 막대한, 거대한
Something that is enormous is extremely large in size or amount.

envelope [énvəlòup] n. 봉투
An envelope is the rectangular paper cover in which you send a letter to someone through the post.

‡ fit [fit] v. (fit/fitted–fit/fitted) (모양·크기가) 맞다; 적절하다; a. 적합한, 알맞은; 건강한; n. ~하게 맞는 것

If something fits, it is the right size and shape to go onto a person's body or onto a particular object.

be left over idiom (필요한 것을 쓰고 난 뒤) 남다

If food or money is left over, it remains when the rest has been eaten or used up.

‡ room [ru:m] n. 자리, 공간; 방, –실

If there is room somewhere, there is enough empty space there for people or things to be fitted in, or for people to move freely or do what they want to.

‡ discover [diskʌ́vər] v. 찾다, 알아내다; 발견하다; 발굴하다

If you discover something that you did not know about before, you become aware of it or learn of it.

‧ toothbrush [tú:θbrʌʃ] n. 칫솔

A toothbrush is a small brush that you use for cleaning your teeth.

복습 case [keis] n. 용기, 통, 상자; (특정한 상황의) 경우; 사건 (toothbrush case n. 칫솔통)

A case is a container that is specially designed to hold or protect something.

‧ stamp [stæmp] n. 우표; 도장; (발을) 쿵쾅거리기; v. 밟다; (도장·스탬프 등을) 찍다

A stamp or a postage stamp is a small piece of paper which you lick and stick on an envelope or package before you post it to pay for the cost of the postage.

‧ airmail [ɛ́ərmeil] n. 항공 우편

Airmail is the system of sending letters, parcels, and goods by air.

‧ insurance [inʃúərəns] n. 보험

Insurance is an arrangement in which you pay money to a company, and they pay money to you if something unpleasant happens to you.

‡fold [fould] v. 접다; (두 손·팔 등을) 끼다; n. 주름; 접힌 부분
If you fold something such as a piece of paper or cloth, you bend it so that one part covers another part, often pressing the edge so that it stays in place.

⋆slot [slat] n. (가느다란) 구멍; v. (가느다란 구멍·자리에) 넣다
A slot is a narrow opening in a machine or container, for example a hole that you put coins in to make a machine work.

limber [límbər] a. 유연한; 재빠른, 경쾌한
A limber person is able to move or bend freely.

⋆straighten [streitn] v. (자세를) 바로 하다; 똑바르게 하다
If you are standing in a relaxed or slightly bent position and then you straighten, you make your back or body straight and upright.

⋆rap [ræp] v. (재빨리) 쾅쾅 두드리다; (큰 소리로 빠르게) 지껄이다; n. (재빨리) 쾅 때리기
If you rap on something or rap it, you hit it with a series of quick blows.

‡dear [diər] n. 얘야; 여보, 당신; int. 이런!, 맙소사!; a. 사랑하는; ~에게
You can call someone dear as a sign of affection.

overheated [òuvərhíːtid] a. 지나치게 더운; (관심·흥분이) 과열된
If something is overheated, it becomes too hot and hotter than necessary or desirable.

marking [máːrkiŋ] n. (도로·차량 등에 그려진) 표시; 무늬
Markings are colored lines, shapes, or patterns on the surface of something, which help to identify it.

⋆valuable [væljuəbl] a. 가치가 큰, 값비싼; 소중한, 귀중한
Valuable objects are objects which are worth a lot of money.

⋆fragile [frǽdʒəl] a. 부서지기 쉬운; 섬세한
Something that is fragile is easily broken or damaged.

‡handle [hændl] v. 들다, 옮기다; (차량·동물·기구 등을) 다루다; 처리하다; n. 손잡이
When you handle something, you hold it or move it with your hands.

* **bump** [bʌmp] n. 부딪치기; 쿵 (하고 부딪치는 소리); v. (~에) 부딪치다; 덜컹거리며 가다
A bump is the action or the dull sound of two heavy objects hitting each other.

* **prove** [pruːv] v. (~임이) 드러나다; 입증하다, 증명하다
If something proves to be true or to have a particular quality, it becomes clear after a period of time that it is true or has that quality.

* **jet** [dʒet] n. 제트기; 분출; v. 급속히 움직이다; 분출하다
A jet is an aircraft that is powered by jet engines.

Stanley the Kite

1. **Why did Mr. Lambchop roll Stanley up when he took the boys out?**

   A. It was too hard for Stanley to walk to places on his own.

   B. It was easier to bring Stanley to places when he was rolled up.

   C. Mr. Lambchop was worried that Stanley would run away.

   D. Mr. Lambchop was worried that Stanley would get blown away by the wind.

2. **Why did Arthur pile many books on top of himself?**

   A. He wanted to clean the bookcase.

   B. He wanted to make his parents worry.

   C. He wanted to be flat like Stanley.

   D. He wanted to read on the floor.

3. What nice thing did Stanley do for Arthur?

A. He let Arthur use him as a kite.

B. He gave Arthur money to buy a kite.

C. He helped Arthur win a kite-flying contest.

D. He made Arthur a big, beautiful kite.

4. What happened while Arthur was eating a hot dog?

A. Someone stole Arthur's kite.

B. Everyone at the park kept watching Stanley fly.

C. Stanley got caught in a tree.

D. The string attached to Stanley got longer and longer.

5. How did Stanley feel after he and Arthur had returned home?

A. He felt a little better.

B. He felt really embarrassed.

C. He still felt very sorry.

D. He still felt angry.

Check Your Reading Speed

1분에 몇 단어를 읽는지 리딩 속도를 측정해보세요.

$$\frac{920 \ words}{reading \ time \ (\quad \ ) \ sec} \times 60 = (\quad \ ) \ WPM$$

Build Your Vocabulary

. **kite** [kait] n. 연
A kite is an object, usually used as a toy, which is flown in the air.

jostle [dʒasl] v. 거칠게 밀치다; n. 충돌
If people jostle you, they bump against you or push you in a way that annoys you, usually because you are in a crowd and they are trying to get past you.

speed [spiːd] v. 빨리 가다; 더 빠르게 하다; n. 속도 (speeding a. 고속으로 움직이는)
Someone who is speeding is driving a vehicle faster than the legal speed limit.

. **accidental** [æksədéntl] a. 우연한, 돌발적인 (accidentally ad. 우연히, 뜻하지 않게)
An accidental event happens by chance or as the result of an accident, and is not deliberately intended.

knock [nak] v. 치다, 부딪치다; (문 등을) 두드리다; n. 문 두드리는 소리; 부딪침
(knock down idiom ~를 때려눕히다)
If someone or something knocks you down, they hit or push you so that you fall to the ground or the floor.

discover [diskʌ́vər] v. 찾다, 알아내다; 발견하다; 발굴하다
If you discover something that you did not know about before, you become aware of it or learn of it.

30

roll [roul] v. (둥글게) 말다; 구르다, 굴러가다; n. 구르기; 굴리기 (unroll v. 펼치다, 펼쳐지다)
If you roll something flexible into a cylinder or a ball, you form it into a cylinder or a ball by wrapping it several times around itself or by shaping it between your hands.

tie [tai] v. (끈 등으로) 묶다; 결부시키다; n. 끈; (강한) 유대
If you tie two things together or tie them, you fasten them together with a knot.

string [striŋ] n. 끈, 줄; 일련; v. 묶다, 매달다; (실 등에) 꿰다
String is thin rope made of twisted threads, used for tying things together or tying up parcels.

loop [luːp] n. 고리 (모양의 밧줄·전선 등); v. 고리 모양을 만들다
A loop is a curved or circular shape in something long, for example in a piece of string.

parcel [páːrsəl] n. 소포; (선물 등의) 꾸러미
A parcel is something wrapped in paper, usually so that it can be sent to someone by post.

college [kálidʒ] n. 대학(교)
A college is an institution where students study for degrees and where academic research is done.

wallpaper [wɔ́ːlpèipər] n. 벽지; v. 벽지를 바르다
Wallpaper is thick colored or patterned paper that is used for covering and decorating the walls of rooms.

decorate [dékərèit] v. 실내장식을 하다; 꾸미다; (훈장을) 수여하다
If you decorate a room or the inside of a building, you put new paint or wallpaper on the walls and ceiling, and paint the woodwork.

undo [ʌndúː] v. (undid-undone) (잠기거나 묶인 것을) 풀다
If you undo something that is closed, tied, or held together, or if you undo the thing holding it, you loosen or remove the thing holding it.

feller [félər] n. (= fellow) 녀석, 친구
You can refer to a man as a feller.

phooey [fuːi] int. 쳇!, 흥! (경멸·의혹·실망 등을 나타내는 소리)
Phooey can be used for showing that you are annoyed or disappointed, or that you do not believe something.

apologize [əpálədʒàiz] v. 사과하다
When you apologize to someone, you say that you are sorry that you have hurt them or caused trouble for them.

rude [ruːd] a. 무례한, 버릇없는; (나쁜 일이) 예상치 못한 (rudeness n. 버릇없음, 무례함)
When people are rude, they act in an impolite way toward other people or say impolite things about them.

blush [blʌʃ] v. 얼굴을 붉히다; ~에 부끄러워하다; n. 얼굴이 붉어짐
When you blush, your face becomes redder than usual because you are ashamed or embarrassed.

set out idiom (여행을) 시작하다; ~을 진열하다
If you set out, you leave a place and begin a journey, especially a long journey.

hardly [háːrdli] ad. 거의 ~아니다; ~하자마자; 거의 ~할 수가 없다
You use hardly to modify a statement when you want to say that it is almost not true or almost does not happen at all.

edge [edʒ] n. 끝, 가장자리; 우위; v. 조금씩 움직이다; 테두리를 두르다
The edge of something is the place or line where it stops, or the part of it that is furthest from the middle.

soak [souk] v. 흠뻑 적시다; (액체 속에 푹) 담그다; n. (액체 속에) 담그기
(soaked a. 흠뻑 젖은)
If someone or something gets soaked or soaked through, water or some other liquid makes them extremely wet.

bookcase [búkkeis] n. 책장, 책꽂이
A bookcase is a piece of furniture with shelves that you keep books on.

pile [pail] v. (차곡차곡) 쌓다; 우르르 가다; n. 쌓아 놓은 것, 더미; 무더기
If you pile things somewhere, you put them there so that they form a mass.

★ **volume** [váljuːm] n. 책; 권; 용량, 용적
A volume is a book.

복습 **jealous** [dʒéləs] a. 질투하는; 시샘하는
If you are jealous of another person's possessions or qualities, you feel angry or bitter because you do not have them.

after all idiom 어쨌든; (예상과는 달리) 결국에는
You use after all when introducing a statement which supports or helps explain something you have just said.

★ **windy** [wíndi] a. 바람이 많이 부는
If it is windy, the wind is blowing a lot.

복습 **enormous** [inɔ́ːrməs] a. 막대한, 거대한
Something that is enormous is extremely large in size or amount.

★ **tail** [teil] n. (~의) 꼬리; (동물의) 꼬리; 끝부분; v. 미행하다
You can use tail to refer to the end or back of something, especially something long and thin.

복습 **sigh** [sai] v. 한숨을 쉬다, 한숨짓다; 탄식하듯 말하다; n. 한숨
When you sigh, you let out a deep breath, as a way of expressing feelings such as disappointment, tiredness, or pleasure.

★ **someday** [sʌ́mdei] ad. (미래의) 언젠가
Someday means at a date in the future that is unknown or that has not yet been decided.

★ **contest** [kántest] ① n. 대회, 시합 ② v. 이의를 제기하다; 경쟁을 벌이다
A contest is a competition or game in which people try to win.

spool [spuːl] n. 실패; v. (실패 같은 것에) 감다
A spool is a round object onto which thread, tape, or film can be wound, especially before it is put into a machine.

★ **attach** [ətǽtʃ] v. 붙이다, 달다; 첨부하다; 연관되다
If you attach something to an object, you join it or fasten it to the object.

* **sideways** [sáidwèiz] ad. 옆으로; 옆에서
Sideways means in a direction to the left or right, not forward or backward.

get up idiom (속도 등을) 높이다; 일어나다, 일어서다
If you get up speed, you start to go faster.

* **breeze** [briːz] n. 산들바람, 미풍; 식은 죽 먹기; v. 경쾌하게 움직이다
A breeze is a gentle wind.

gust [gʌst] n. 세찬 바람, 돌풍; v. (갑자기) 몰아치다
A gust is a short, strong, sudden rush of wind.

* **slip** [slip] v. 슬며시 가다; 미끄러지다; (손에서) 빠져 나가다; n. (작은) 실수; 미끄러짐
If you slip somewhere, you go there quickly and quietly.

* **graceful** [gréisfəl] a. 우아한, 기품 있는 (gracefully ad. 우아하게)
Someone or something that is graceful moves in a smooth and controlled way which is attractive to watch.

* **soar** [sɔːr] v. (하늘 높이) 날아오르다; 솟구치다
If something such as a bird soars into the air, it goes quickly up into the air.

* **sight** [sait] n. 광경, 모습; 시야; 보기, 봄; v. 갑자기 보다
A sight is something that you see.

* **trousers** [tráuzərz] n. 바지
Trousers are a piece of clothing that you wear over your body from the waist downward, and that cover each leg separately.

* **pale** [peil] a. (색깔이) 옅은; 창백한, 핼쑥한; v. 창백해지다
If something is pale, it is very light in color or almost white.

* **still** [stil] a. 가만히 있는, 정지한; ad. 아직(도) (계속해서)
If you stay still, you stay in the same position and do not move.

swoop [swuːp] v. 급강하하다, 위에서 덮치다; 급습하다; n. 급강하; 급습
When a bird or airplane swoops, it suddenly moves downward through the air in a smooth curving movement.

＊ **match** [mætʃ] v. 일치하다; 어울리다; 맞먹다; n. 성냥; 똑같은 것
If something such as an amount or a quality matches with another amount or quality, they are both the same or equal.

zoom [zuːm] v. 쌩 하고 가다; 급등하다; n. (자동차가 빠르게) 쌩 하고 지나가는 소리
If you zoom somewhere, you go there very quickly.

＊ **curve** [kəːrv] v. 곡선으로 나아가다, 곡선을 이루다; n. 곡선
If something curves, it moves in a curve, for example through the air.

＊ **circle** [səːrkl] v. (공중에서) 빙빙 돌다; 에워싸다, 둘러싸다; n. 원형; 동그라미
If an aircraft or a bird circles or circles something, it moves round in a circle in the air.

＊＊ **figure** [fígjər] n. 숫자; 수치; 형체, 형상; (멀리서 흐릿하게 보이는) 사람;
v. 생각하다; 중요하다
A figure is any of the ten written symbols from 0 to 9 that are used to represent a number.

＊ **tired** [taiərd] a. 싫증난, 지긋지긋한; 피로한, 피곤한, 지친
(grow tired of idiom ~에 싫증나다)
If you are tired of something, you do not want it to continue because you are bored of it or unhappy with it.

go on idiom 계속되다
If you go on doing something, you continue an activity without stopping.

show off idiom ~을 자랑하다; 돋보이게 하다
If someone is showing off, they behave in a way that is intended to attract attention or admiration, and that other people often find annoying.

＊ **wedge** [wedʒ] v. (좁은 틈 사이에) 끼워 넣다; 고정시키다; n. 분열의 원인; 쐐기
If you wedge something somewhere, you fit it there tightly.

fork [fɔːrk] n. 여러 갈래로 갈라진 나무; (도로·강 등의) 분기점; 포크; v. 갈라지다, 나뉘다
A fork in a road, path, or river is a point at which it divides into two parts and forms a 'Y' shape.

notice [nóutis] v. 알아채다, 인지하다; 주의하다; n. 신경씀, 주목, 알아챔
If you notice something or someone, you become aware of them.

tangle [tæŋgl] v. 얽히다, 헝클어지다; n. (실·머리카락 등이) 엉킨 것; 엉망인 상태
If something is tangled or tangles, it becomes twisted together in an untidy way.

realize [ríːəlaiz] v. 깨닫다, 알아차리다; 실현하다, 달성하다
If you realize that something is true, you become aware of that fact or understand it.

brush [brʌʃ] v. ～을 스치다; 솔질을 하다; n. 붓; 솔; 비; 붓질, 솔질
If one thing brushes against another or if you brush one thing against another, the first thing touches the second thing lightly while passing it.

stuck [stʌk] a. 움직일 수 없는, 꼼짝 못하는; 갇힌
If something is stuck in a particular position, it is fixed tightly in this position and is unable to move.

branch [brænʧ] n. 나뭇가지; 지사, 분점; v. 갈라지다, 나뉘다
The branches of a tree are the parts that grow out from its trunk and have leaves, flowers, or fruit growing on them.

bedtime [bédtàim] n. 취침 시간, 잠자리에 드는 시간
Your bedtime is the time when you usually go to bed.

cross [krɔːs] a. 짜증난, 약간 화가 난; v. (가로질러) 건너다; n. 십자 기호
Someone who is cross is rather angry or irritated.

go through idiom ～을 겪다; ～을 살펴보다
If you go through something, you experience or suffer it.

phase [feiz] n. (변화·발달의) 단계; v. 단계적으로 하다
A phase is a particular stage in a process or in the gradual development of something.

36

＊ patient [péiʃənt] a. 참을성 있는, 인내심 있는; n. 환자

If you are patient, you stay calm and do not get annoyed.

복습 dear [diər] n. 여보, 당신; 얘야; int. 이런!, 맙소사!; a. 사랑하는; ～에게

You can call someone dear as a sign of affection.

The Museum Thieves

1. Why had Mr. Dart become so gloomy?

A. He had lost his job at the Famous Museum of Art.

B. Nobody wanted to visit his museum anymore.

C. Some of the paintings at his museum had been stolen.

D. The police had suspected him of taking paintings from his museum.

2. What is one reason why the museum guards couldn't catch the sneak thieves?

A. The guards had trouble staying awake all night.

B. The guards had too many other responsibilities.

C. The guards were afraid of the thieves.

D. The guards were much slower than the thieves.

3. **Why did Stanley dress as a shepherdess instead of a cowboy?**

    A. Stanley thought the shepherdess disguise was much prettier.

    B. There were already many cowboy paintings in the main hall.

    C. The cowboy suit didn't fit Stanley well.

    D. The shepherdess disguise fit better with the other paintings in the main hall.

4. **How had the sneak thieves been able to get into the museum so many times without being seen?**

    A. They had climbed through an unlocked window in the main hall.

    B. They had used a trapdoor in the floor of the main hall.

    C. They had walked through the front entrance of the museum when it was pitch-black.

    D. They had entered through an opening in the roof of the museum.

5. **What did Stanley do as the sneak thieves were looking at the world's most expensive painting?**

    A. He started to cry because he was scared.

    B. He yelled to alert the police and Mr. Dart.

    C. He told the thieves to go home.

    D. He jumped on the thieves and handcuffed them.

Check Your Reading Speed

1분에 몇 단어를 읽는지 리딩 속도를 측정해보세요.

$$\frac{1,423 \text{ words}}{\text{reading time (} \quad \text{) sec}} \times 60 = (\quad) \text{ WPM}$$

Build Your Vocabulary

* **director** [diréktər] n. (활동·부서 등의) 책임자; (회사의) 임원
In some organizations and public authorities, the person in charge is referred to as the director.

* **downtown** [dauntáun] a. 도심에 있는; ad. 시내에; n. 도심지; 상업 지구
Downtown places are in or toward the center of a large town or city, where the shops and places of business are.

^{복습}**notice** [nóutis] v. 알아채다, 인지하다; 주의하다; n. 신경씀, 주목, 알아챔
If you notice something or someone, you become aware of them.

* **ordinary** [ɔ́:rdənèri] a. 보통의, 일상적인; 평범한 (ordinarily ad. 보통 때는, 대개는)
If you say what is ordinarily the case, you are saying what is normally the case.

^{복습}**cheerful** [tʃíərfəl] a. 발랄한, 쾌활한; 쾌적한
Someone who is cheerful is happy and shows this in their behavior.

* **gloomy** [glú:mi] a. 우울한, 침울한; 어둑어둑한; 음울한
If people are gloomy, they are unhappy and have no hope.

^{복습}**steal** [sti:l] v. (stole—stolen) 훔치다, 도둑질하다; 살며시 움직이다
If you steal something from someone, you take it away from them without their permission and without intending to return it.

* **wit** [wit] n. (pl.) 지혜; 기지, 재치 (at one's wits' end idiom 어찌할 바를 몰라)
If you say that you are at your wits' end, you are emphasizing that you are so worried and exhausted by problems or difficulties that you do not know what to do next.

복습 **dear** [diər] int. 이런!, 맙소사!; n. 얘야; 여보, 당신; a. 사랑하는; ~에게
You can use dear in expressions such as 'oh dear,' 'dear me,' and 'dear, dear' when you are sad, disappointed, or surprised about something.

* **chief** [ʧiːf] n. (조직·집단의) 장(長); a. (계급·직급상) 최고위자인
The chief of an organization is the person who is in charge of it.

* **suspect** [səspékt] v. 의심하다; 수상쩍어 하다; n. 용의자
If you suspect someone of doing a dishonest or unpleasant, you believe that they probably did it.

* **gang** [gæŋ] n. 범죄 조직; 친구들 무리
A gang is a group of criminals who work together to commit crimes.

sneak [sniːk] a. 은밀한, 몰래 하는; 기습적인; v. 몰래 하다; 살금살금 가다
(sneak thief n. 좀도둑, 빈집털이)
A sneak thief is a person who steals whatever is readily available without using violence or forcibly breaking into buildings.

* **meanwhile** [míːnwàil] ad. 한편; (다른 일이 일어나고 있는) 그 동안에
You use meanwhile to introduce a different aspect of a particular situation, especially one that is completely opposite to the one previously mentioned.

복습 **policeman** [pəlíːsmən] n. (pl. policemen) 경찰관
A policeman is a man who is a member of the police force.

* **ball** [bɔːl] n. (큰 규모의) 무도회; 공; v. 동그랗게 만들다
A ball is a large formal social event at which people dance.

복습 **sign** [sain] n. 표지판, 간판; 징후; 몸짓; v. 서명하다; 신호를 보내다
A sign is a piece of wood, metal, or plastic with words or pictures on it. Signs give you information about something, or give you a warning or an instruction.

‡ **guard** [gɑːrd] n. 경비 요원; 감시, 경호, 경비; v. 지키다, 보호하다, 경비를 보다; 감시하다
A guard is a specially organized group of people, such as soldiers or policemen, who protect or watch someone or something.

‡ **duty** [djúːti] n. 직무, 임무; (도덕적·법률적) 의무 (on duty idiom 근무 중인)
If someone is on duty, they are working.

⁎ **hopeless** [hóuplis] a. 가망 없는, 절망적인; 엉망인
Someone or something that is hopeless is certain to fail or be unsuccessful.

⁎ **electric** [iléktrik] a. 전기의; 전기를 이용하는
An electric device or machine works by means of electricity, rather than using some other source of power.

⁎ **bulb** [bʌlb] n. (= light bulb) 전구
A bulb is the glass part of an electric lamp, which gives out light when electricity passes through it.

give out idiom (열·빛 등을) 내다
To give out something such as light or heat means to produce it.

‡‡ **permit** [pərmít] v. 허락하다; n. 허가증 (permission n. 허락, 허가)
If someone gives you permission to do something, they say that they will allow you to do it.

put to work idiom ~에게 일을 시키다
If you put someone to work, you make them start doing something.

⁎ **nap** [næp] n. 잠깐 잠, 낮잠; v. 잠깐 자다, 낮잠을 자다
If you have a nap, you have a short sleep, usually during the day.

⁎ **beard** [biərd] n. (턱)수염 (bearded a. 수염이 있는)
A man's beard is the hair that grows on his chin and cheeks.

floppy [flápi] a. 헐렁한, 늘어진; 딱딱하지 않은
Something that is floppy is loose rather than stiff, and tends to hang downward.

* **couch** [kauʧ] n. 긴 의자, 소파
A couch is a long, comfortable seat for two or three people.

‡ **frame** [freim] n. 틀, 액자; (가구·건물·차량 등의) 뼈대; v. 액자에 넣다, 테를 두르다
The frame of a picture or mirror is the wood, metal, or plastic that is fitted around it, especially when it is displayed or hung on a wall.

‡ **opposite** [ápəzit] a. 건너편의; 맞은편의; (정)반대의
The opposite side or part of something is the side or part that is furthest away from you.

* **disguise** [disgáiz] n. 변장; v. 위장하다, 숨기다; 변장하다
If you are in disguise, you are not wearing your usual clothes or you have altered your appearance in other ways, so that people will not recognize you.

‡ **suit** [su:t] n. (특정한 활동 때 입는) 옷; 정장; v. 어울리다; ~에게 편리하다
A particular type of suit is a piece of clothing that you wear for a particular activity.

복습 **tie** [tai] v. (끈 등으로) 묶다; 결부시키다; n. 끈; (강한) 유대
If you tie two things together or tie them, you fasten them together with a knot.

‡ **recognize** [rékəgnàiz] v. 알아보다; 인식하다; 공인하다
If you recognize someone or something, you know who that person is or what that thing is.

* **closet** [klázit] n. 벽장
A closet is a piece of furniture with doors at the front and shelves inside, which is used for storing things.

sash [sæʃ] n. (옷의 일부로 몸에 두르는) 허리띠
A sash is a long piece of cloth which people wear round their waist or over one shoulder, especially with formal or official clothes.

* **pointed** [pɔ́intid] a. (끝이) 뾰족한
Something that is pointed has a point at one end.

★ straw [strɔ:] n. 짚, 밀짚; 빨대 (straw hat n. 밀짚모자)
Straw consists of the dried, yellowish stalks from crops such as wheat or barley.

복습 match [mæʧ] v. 어울리다; 일치하다; 맞먹다; n. 성냥; 똑같은 것
If something of a particular color or design matches another thing, they have the same color or design, or have a pleasing appearance when they are used together.

wig [wig] n. 가발
A wig is a covering of false hair which you wear on your head.

☆ stick [stik] n. 막대기, 나무토막; v. 찌르다, 박다; 붙이다, 붙다
A stick is a long thin piece of wood which is used for a particular purpose.

★ blond [bland] a. (사람이) 금발 머리인
A man who has blond hair has pale-colored hair.

ringlet [ríŋlit] n. (pl.) 곱슬머리
Ringlets are long curls of hair that hang down.

복습 curve [kə:rv] v. 곡선으로 나아가다, 곡선을 이루다; n. 곡선
If something curves, or if someone or something curves it, it has the shape of a curve.

shepherdess [ʃépərdis] n. 여자 양치기
A shepherdess is a woman whose job is to look after sheep.

복복 belong [bilɔ́:ŋ] v. 제자리에 있다; 소속감을 느끼다; ~에 속하다
If a person or thing belongs in a particular place or situation, that is where they should be.

★ disgust [disgʌ́st] v. 혐오감을 유발하다, 역겹게 하다; n. 혐오감, 역겨움
(disgusted a. 혐오감을 느끼는, 넌더리를 내는)
If you are disgusted, you feel a strong sense of dislike and disapproval at something.

^복^습hardly [háːrdli] ad. 거의 ~할 수가 없다; 거의 ~아니다; ~하자마자
When you say you can hardly do something, you are emphasizing that it is very difficult for you to do it.

[★][★]sport [spɔːrt] n. 싹싹한 사람, 좋은 녀석; 스포츠; v. 자랑스럽게 보이다
If you say that someone is a sport or a good sport, you mean that they cope with a difficult situation or teasing in a cheerful way.

[★][★]clever [klévər] a. 기발한, 재치 있는; 영리한, 똑똑한 (cleverly ad. 솜씨 좋게)
A clever idea, book, or invention is extremely effective and shows the skill of the people involved.

spike [spaik] n. 못; 급등, 급증; v. (뾰족한 것으로) 찌르다; 못을 박다
A spike is a long piece of metal with a sharp point.

^복^습fit [fit] n. ~하게 맞는 것; v. (모양·크기가) 맞다; 적절하다; a. 적합한, 알맞은; 건강한
If something is a good fit, it fits well.

[★][★]except [iksépt] prep. (~을) 제외하고는
You use except to introduce the only thing or person that a statement does not apply to, or a fact that prevents a statement from being completely true.

_★fierce [fiərs] a. 사나운, 험악한; 격렬한, 맹렬한
A fierce animal or person is very aggressive or angry.

_★faraway [fáːrəwei] a. 생각이 딴 데 가 있는 듯한; 멀리 떨어진, 먼
If you have a faraway look, you seem remote from your immediate surroundings.

^복^습stare [stɛər] v. 빤히 쳐다보다, 응시하다; n. 빤히 쳐다보기, 응시
If you stare at someone or something, you look at them for a long time.

take care of idiom ~을 처리하다; ~을 돌보다
To take care of a problem, task, or situation means to deal with it.

make out idiom ~을 알아보다; 주장하다
If you make someone or something out, you see, hear, or understand them with difficulty.

winged [wiŋd] a. 날개가 있는, 날개 달린; 날개가 ~한
A winged insect or other creature has wings.

tired [taiərd] a. 피로한, 피곤한, 지친; 싫증난, 지긋지긋한
If you are tired, you feel that you want to rest or sleep.

pitch-dark [piʧ-dáːrk] a. 칠흑같이 어두운
If a place or the night is pitch-dark, it is extremely dark.

* **absolute** [ǽbsəlùːt] a. 완전한, 완벽한; 확실한 (absolutely ad. 극도로, 굉장히; 틀림없이)
Absolutely means totally and completely.

prickle [prikl] v. (무서움 · 흥분 등으로) (머리털이) 곤두서다; 까칠거리다;
n. (작은) 가시; 오싹해짐
If your skin prickles, it feels as if a lot of small sharp points are being stuck into it, either because of something touching it or because you feel a strong emotion.

beneath [biníːθ] prep. 아래에
Something that is beneath another thing is under the other thing.

* **curl** [kəːrl] n. 곱슬곱슬한 머리카락; v. (둥그렇게) 감다; 곱슬곱슬하다
If you have curls, your hair is in the form of tight curves and spirals.

creak [kriːk] v. 삐걱거리다; n. 삐걱거리는 소리
If something creaks, it makes a short, high-pitched sound when it moves.

* **tiny** [táini] a. 아주 작은
Something or someone that is tiny is extremely small.

* **glow** [glou] n. (은은한) 불빛; 홍조; v. 빛나다, 타다; (얼굴이) 상기되다
A glow is a dull, steady light, for example the light produced by a fire when there are no flames.

trapdoor [trǽpdɔːr] n. (바닥 · 천장에 나 있는) 작은 문
A trapdoor is a small horizontal door in a floor, a ceiling, or on a stage.

all at once idiom 갑자기; 동시에
If something happens all at once, it happens suddenly, often when you are not expecting it to happen.

˚ **entrance** [éntrəns] n. 입구, 문; 입장, 등장
The entrance to a place is the way into it, for example a door or gate.

복습 **still** [stil] a. 가만히 있는, 정지한; ad. 아직(도) (계속해서)
If you stay still, you stay in the same position and do not move.

˚ **rob** [rab] v. (사람·장소를) 도둑질하다 (robber n. 강도)
A robber is someone who steals money or property from a bank, a shop, or a vehicle, often by using force or threats.

pull a job idiom 도둑질하다
To pull a job means to carry out a crime, especially a robbery.

sensational [senséiʃənl] a. 세상을 놀라게 하는, 선풍적인; 매우 훌륭한
A sensational result, event, or situation is so remarkable that it causes great excitement and interest.

whilst [wailst] conj. ~하는 동안, 사이
If something happens whilst something else is happening, the two things are happening at the same time.

₊ **civilize** [sívəlàiz] v. 개화하다; (태도를) 세련되게 하다 (civilized a. 문명화된)
If you describe a society as civilized, you mean that it is advanced and has sensible laws and customs.

˚ **community** [kəmjúːnəti] n. 지역 사회, 주민; 공동체
The community is all the people who live in a particular area or place.

₊ **lantern** [læntərn] n. 손전등
A lantern is a lamp in a metal frame with glass sides and with a handle on top so you can carry it.

₊ **capture** [kǽpʧər] v. 붙잡다; 포획하다; (관심·상상력·흥미를) 사로잡다; n. 포획; 구금
If you capture someone or something, you catch them, especially in a war.

‡ frighten [fraitn] v. 겁먹게 하다, 놀라게 하다 (frightened a. 겁먹은, 무서워하는)
If something or someone frightens you, they cause you to suddenly feel afraid, anxious, or nervous.

‡ scare [skɛər] v. 겁주다, 놀라게 하다; 무서워하다; n. 불안(감); 놀람, 공포
(scared a. 무서워하는, 겁먹은)
If you are scared of someone or something, you are frightened of them.

in time idiom 제때에, 시간 맞춰, 늦지 않게
If you are in time for a particular event, you are not too late for it.

★ furious [fjúəriəs] a. 몹시 화가 난; 맹렬한
Someone who is furious is extremely angry.

★ terrify [térəfài] v. (몹시) 무섭게 하다 (terrifying a. 겁나게 하는; 무서운)
If something is terrifying, it makes you very frightened.

★ yell [jel] v. 고함치다, 소리 지르다; n. 고함, 외침
If you yell, you shout loudly, usually because you are excited, angry, or in pain.

★ quiver [kwívər] v. (가볍게) 떨다; n. (몸의 일부가) 떨림; 가벼운 전율
(quivery a. 흔들리는, 떨리는)
If you say that someone or their voice is quivering with an emotion such as rage or excitement, you mean that they are strongly affected by this emotion and show it in their appearance or voice.

‡ rest [rest] n. 휴식; 나머지; v. 쉬다; 놓이다, (~에) 있다
If you get some rest or have a rest, you do not do anything active for a time.

‡ rush [rʌʃ] v. 급히 움직이다; 서두르다; n. (강한 감정이) 치밀어 오름; 혼잡, 분주함
If you rush somewhere, you go there quickly.

‡ arrest [ərést] v. 체포하다; 막다; n. 체포; 저지, 정지
If the police arrest you, they take charge of you and take you to a police station, because they believe you may have committed a crime.

48

be mixed up idiom 혼란해지다, 뭐가 뭔지 모르게 되다
If you are mixed up, you are confused, often because of emotional or social problems.

❊ **joke** [dʒouk] n. 농담; 웃음거리; v. 농담하다, 재미있는 이야기를 하다
A joke is something that is said or done to make you laugh, for example a funny story.

put up idiom (싸움·시합에서 어떤 기량·결의 등을) 보이다
If you put up a fight or put up resistance in a game or an argument, you resist strongly or fight hard.

handcuff [hǽndkʌ̀f] v. 수갑을 채우다; n. 수갑
If you handcuff someone, you put handcuffs around their wrists.

⁎ **jail** [dʒeil] n. 교도소, 감옥; v. 수감하다
A jail is a place where criminals are kept in order to punish them, or where people waiting to be tried are kept.

Arthur's Good Idea

1. **Why did people begin to make fun of Stanley?**

   A. They were jealous of all the attention he had been getting..

   B. They thought it was funny that he looked so different.

   C. They didn't like his style of clothing.

   D. They wanted Stanley to laugh at their jokes.

2. **Why wasn't Stanley happy anymore?**

   A. He was tired of being normal.

   B. He was tired of being ignored.

   C. He didn't want to be famous anymore.

   D. He didn't want to be flat anymore.

3. What did Arthur do to help Stanley become round again?

A. He used a bicycle pump to get air into Stanley.

B. He used a bicycle pump to remove air from Stanley.

C. He used a hose to pump water for Stanley to drink.

D. He used a hose to help Stanley breathe.

4. How did Stanley finally get his right foot to become round again?

A. He had Arthur pump more air into him.

B. He shook his right foot a few times.

C. He squeezed his left foot twice.

D. He stomped his feet several times.

5. What did Mr. and Mrs. Lambchop do when they realized Stanley was no longer flat?

A. They made Stanley and Arthur go right back to bed.

B. They scolded Stanley and Arthur for not being more careful.

C. They had a small family celebration.

D. They told Stanley that they wished he were flat again.

Check Your Reading Speed

1분에 몇 단어를 읽는지 리딩 속도를 측정해보세요.

$$\frac{876 \text{ words}}{\text{reading time ( ) sec}} \times 60 = (\qquad) \text{ WPM}$$

Build Your Vocabulary

^복^습 stare [stɛər] v. 빤히 쳐다보다, 응시하다; n. 빤히 쳐다보기, 응시
If you stare at someone or something, you look at them for a long time.

· whisper [hwíspər] v. 속삭이다, 소곤거리다; 은밀히 말하다; n. 속삭임, 소곤거리는 소리
When you whisper, you say something very quietly, using your breath rather than your throat, so that only one person can hear you.

^복^습 sneak [sni:k] a. 은밀한, 몰래 하는; 기습적인; v. 몰래 하다; 살금살금 가다
(sneak thief n. 좀도둑, 빈집털이)
A sneak thief is a person who steals whatever is readily available without using violence or forcibly breaking into buildings.

⁎ pleasant [plézənt] a. 즐거운, 기분 좋은; 상냥한
Something that is pleasant is nice, enjoyable, or attractive.

make fun of idiom ~을 놀리다, 비웃다
If you make fun of someone or something, you laugh at them, tease them, or make jokes about them in a way that causes them to seem ridiculous.

skinny [skíni] a. 깡마른, 비쩍 마른
A skinny person is extremely thin, often in a way that you find unattractive.

^복^습 rude [ru:d] a. 무례한, 버릇없는; (나쁜 일이) 예상치 못한
When people are rude, they act in an impolite way toward other people or say impolite things about them.

shame [ʃeim] n. 수치(심), 창피; 애석한 일; v. 창피스럽게 하다; 망신시키다
You can use shame in expressions such as shame on you and shame on him to indicate that someone ought to feel shame for something they have said or done.

religion [rilídʒən] n. 종교
Religion is belief in a god or gods and the activities that are connected with this belief, such as praying or worshipping in a church or temple.

for that matter idiom 그 문제라면, 그 점에 대해서는
You can use for that matter to emphasize that the remark you are making is true in the same way as your previous, similar remark.

creep [kriːp] v. (crept–crept) 살금살금 움직이다; 기다; n. 너무 싫은 사람
When people or animals creep somewhere, they move quietly and slowly.

kneel [niːl] v. (knelt–knelt) 무릎을 꿇다
When you kneel, you bend your legs so that your knees are touching the ground.

tangle [tæŋgl] v. 얽히다, 헝클어지다; n. (실·머리카락 등이) 엉킨 것; 엉망인 상태
If something is tangled or tangles, it becomes twisted together in an untidy way.

kite [kait] n. 연
A kite is an object, usually used as a toy, which is flown in the air.

skip it idiom 그냥 넘어가
If you say 'skip it' to someone, you tell them impolitely that you do not want to talk about something or repeat what you have said.

tired [taiərd] a. 싫증난, 지긋지긋한; 피로한, 피곤한, 지친
If you are tired of something, you do not want it to continue because you are bored of it or unhappy with it.

regular [régjulər] a. 일반적인, 평범한; 보통의; 규칙적인, 정기적인
Regular is used to mean 'normal.'

^{복습} **go on** idiom 계속되다
If you go on doing something, you continue an activity without stopping.

sheet [ʃiːt] n. (침대) 시트; (종이) 한 장
A sheet is a large rectangular piece of cotton or other cloth that you sleep on or cover yourself with in a bed.

folk [fouk] n. (pl.) 부모; (pl.) (일반적인) 사람들; (pl.) 여러분, 얘들아
You can refer to your close family, especially your mother and father, as your folks.

storage [stɔ́ːridʒ] n. 저장, 보관; 저장고, 보관소 (storage box n. 보관함)
If you refer to the storage of something, you mean that it is kept in a special place until it is needed.

rummage [rʌ́midʒ] v. 뒤지다; n. 뒤지기
If you rummage through something, you search for something you want by moving things around in a careless or hurried way.

fling [fliŋ] v. (flung-flung) (거칠게) 내던지다; (머리·팔 등을) 휘두르다; n. (한바탕) 즐기기
If you fling something somewhere, you throw it there using a lot of force.

pump [pʌmp] n. 펌프; v. (펌프로) 퍼 올리다; (거세게) 솟구치다
(bicycle pump n. 자전거 공기 주입 펌프)
A pump is a machine or device that is used to force a liquid or gas to flow in a particular direction.

take it easy idiom 진정해라; 쉬엄쉬엄 해라
When you are saying 'take it easy' to someone, you tell them to relax and avoid working too hard or doing too much.

hose [houz] n. 호스; v. 호스로 물을 뿌리다
A hose is a long, flexible pipe made of rubber or plastic. It is used for carrying water to a garden or a fire.

clamp [klæmp] v. 꽉 물다; 죔쇠로 고정시키다; n. 죔쇠
To clamp something in a particular place means to put it or hold it there firmly and tightly.

wiggle [wígl] v. 꿈틀꿈틀 움직이다; n. 꿈틀꿈틀 움직이기
If you wiggle something or if it wiggles, it moves up and down or from side to side in small quick movements.

except [iksépt] prep. (~을) 제외하고는
You use except to introduce the only thing or person that a statement does not apply to, or a fact that prevents a statement from being completely true.

cheek [ʧiːk] n. 뺨, 볼
Your cheeks are the sides of your face below your eyes.

bulge [bʌldʒ] v. 툭 불거져 나오다; 가득 차다; n. 툭 튀어 나온 것, 불룩한 것
If something such as a person's stomach bulges, it sticks out.

signal [sígnəl] n. 신호; 징조; v. (동작·소리로) 신호를 보내다; 암시하다
A signal is a gesture, sound, or action which is intended to give a particular message to the person who sees or hears it.

swell [swel] v. 불룩해지다; 증가하다; n. 증가, 팽창
If something such as a part of your body swells, it becomes larger and rounder than normal.

spread [spred] v. (spread-spread) (팔·다리 등을) 펴다, 뻗다; 확산되다; n. 확산, 전파
If you spread your arms, hands, fingers, or legs, you stretch them out until they are far apart.

pajama [pədʒáːmə] n. (pl.) (바지와 상의로 된) 잠옷
A pair of pajamas consists of loose trousers and a loose jacket that people, especially men, wear in bed.

burst [bəːrst] v. (~으로) 터질 듯하다; 터지다, 파열하다; 불쑥 움직이다;
n. (갑자기) 한바탕 ~을 함
If something bursts or if you burst it, it suddenly breaks open or splits open and the air or other substance inside it comes out.

pop [pap] n. 펑 (하고 터지는 소리); v. 펑 하는 소리가 나다; 불쑥 나타나다
Pop is used to represent a short sharp sound, for example the sound made by bursting a balloon or by pulling a cork out of a bottle.

‡ round [raund] v. 둥글게 만들다; (모퉁이·커브 등을) 돌다; a. 둥근, 동그란
If you round something, you make it into a shape like a circle or ball.

whoosh [hwuːʃ] v. (아주 빠르게) 휙 하고 지나가다; n. 쉭 하는 소리
People sometimes say 'whoosh' when they are emphasizing the fact that
something happens very suddenly or very fast.

복습 match [mætʃ] v. 일치하다; 어울리다; 맞먹다; n. 성냥; 똑같은 것
If something such as an amount or a quality matches with another
amount or quality, they are both the same or equal.

used to idiom ~하곤 했다
If something used to be done or used to be the case, it was done
regularly in the past or was the case in the past.

₊ stride [straid] v. (strode–stridden) 성큼성큼 걷다; n. 걸음; 걸음걸이
If you stride somewhere, you walk there with quick, long steps.

복습 notice [nóutis] v. 알아채다, 인지하다; 주의하다; n. 신경씀, 주목, 알아챔
If you notice something or someone, you become aware of them.

₊ terrible [térəbl] a. 극심한; 끔찍한, 소름끼치는; 형편없는 (terribly ad. 몹시, 극심하게)
You use terrible to emphasize the great extent or degree of something.

‡ celebrate [séləbrèit] v. 기념하다, 축하하다
If you celebrate, you do something enjoyable because of a special
occasion or to mark someone's success.

‡ occasion [əkéiʒən] n. 경우, 기회; 특별한 일, 행사
An occasion is a time when something happens, or a case of it happening.

₊ toast [toust] n. 건배, 축배; v. 노릇노릇하게 하다; 건배하다
When you drink a toast to someone or something, you drink some wine
or another alcoholic drink as a symbolic gesture, in order to show your
appreciation of them or to wish them success.

복습 clever [klévər] a. 기발한, 재치 있는; 영리한, 똑똑한 (cleverness n. 솜씨 좋음)
A clever idea, book, or invention is extremely effective and shows the
skill of the people involved.

* **tuck** [tʌk] v. (따뜻하게) 단단히 덮어 주다; 집어 넣다; 밀어넣다; n. 주름, 단
(tuck in idiom ~에게 이불을 잘 덮어 주다)
If you tuck in someone, especially a child, you cover them comfortably
in bed by pulling the covers around them.

* **tiring** [táiəriŋ] a. 피곤하게 하는, 피곤한
If you describe something as tiring, you mean that it makes you tired so
that you want to rest or sleep.

1장 커다란 게시판

아침 식사가 준비되었습니다.

"내가 가서 아이들을 깨울게요." 램찹 부인(Mrs. Lambchop)이 그녀의 남편 조지 램찹(George Lambchop)에게 말했습니다. 바로 그때 그들의 막내아들 아서(Arthur)가 자신의 형, 스탠리(Stanley)와 함께 쓰는 침실에서 외쳤습니다.

"헤이(Hey)! 와서 좀 보세요! 여기요!"

램찹 부부 두 사람은 모두 예의범절과 조심성 있는 말투를 무척이나 좋아했습니다. "건초(Hay)는 말을 위한 거란다, 아서, 사람을 위한 게 아니야." 램찹 씨가 말하면서 그들은 침실로 들어갔습니다. "그 사실을 기억하도록 하려무나."

"죄송해요." 아서가 말했습니다. "하지만 좀 보세요!"

그가 스탠리의 침대를 가리켰습니다. 램찹 씨가 아이들이 사진과 메시지 그리고 지도를 꽂을 수 있도록 지난 크리스마스에 그들에게 주었던 거대한 게시판이 침대를 가로지르며 놓여 있었습니다. 그것은, 밤사이에, 스탠리의 위로 떨어졌던 것입니다.

하지만 스탠리는 다치지 않았습니다. 사실, 그가 자신의 동생이 외치는 소리 때문에 깨지 않았더라면 그는 여전히 자고 있었을 것입니다.

"도대체 무슨 일이에요?" 그가 거대한 게시판 밑에서 명랑하게 외쳤습니다.

램찹 부부는 서둘러서 그것을 침대에서 들어 올렸습니다.

"맙소사!" 램찹 부인이 말했습니다.

"이럴 수가!" 아서가 말했습니다. "스탠리 형이 납작해졌어요!"

"팬케이크처럼 말이야." 램찹 씨가 말했습니다. "내가 여태껏 본 것 중에 가장 놀라운 일이야."

"모두 일단 아침을 먹어요." 램찹 부인이 말했습니다. "그다음에 스탠리와 내가 가서 댄 의사 선생님(Dr. Dan)을 만나 선생님이 뭐라고 하는지 들어 볼게요."

자신의 진료실에서, 댄 의사 선생님은 스탠리의 몸 곳곳을 진찰했습니다.

"네 기분은 어떠니?" 그가 물었습니다. "많이 아프거나 그러니?"

"전 일어난 후에 잠깐 좀 간지러웠어요." 스탠리 램찹이 말했습니다. "하지만 전 지금은 괜찮아요."

"흠, 그건 이런 경우에 대부분 일어나는 증상이란다." 댄 의사 선생님이 말했습니다.

"우리는 단지 이 어린 친구를 잘 관찰하기만 하면 될 것 같군요." 그가 진찰을 끝냈을 때 말했습니다. "때때로 우리 의사들은, 우리의 모든 수년간의 훈련과 경험에도 불구하고, 우리가 아는 것이 얼마나 없는지에 대해서 놀랄 수밖에 없곤 하죠."

램찹 부인은 그녀가 생각하기에 스탠리의 옷이 이제 재단사에 의해 수선되어야 할 것 같다고 말했고, 그래서 댄 선생님은 그의 간호사에게 스탠리의 치수를 재라고 말했습니다.

램찹 부인은 그것들을 받아 적었습니다.

스탠리는 4피트의 키에, 약 1피트 정도의 폭이었고, 0.5인치의 두께가 되었습니다.

2장 납작해진다는 것

스탠리가 납작해졌다는 것에 익숙해지자, 그는 그 사실을 즐겼습니다. 그는 심지어 문이 닫혔을 때도, 그냥 누워서 아래에 난 틈으로 미끄러져 지나가서, 방을 들락날락할 수 있었습니다.

램찹 부부는 그게 우스꽝스럽다고 말했지만, 그들은 그를 꽤 자랑스러워했습니다.

아서는 질투가 나서 문 아래로 미끄러져 들어가려고 했지만, 그는 그저 자신의 머리를 쿵 하고 부딪힐 뿐이었습니다.

납작해진다는 것은 또한, 스탠리가 깨닫기로는, 도움이 되기도 했습니다.

그가 어느 오후에 램찹 부인과 함께 산책하고 있었을 때 그녀가 가장 좋아하는 반지가 그녀의 손가락에서 빠져나갔습니다. 반지는 보도를 지나 굴러가서 깊고, 어두운 통로를 덮은 격자 뚜껑의 창살 사이로 떨어졌습니다. 램찹 부인은 울기 시작했습니다.

"제게 좋은 생각이 있어요." 스탠리가 말했습니다.

그는 자신의 신발에서 운동화 끈을 빼냈고 그의 주머니에서 여분의 운동화 끈 한 쌍을 꺼내 그것을 모두 묶어 하나의 긴 끈을 만들었습니다. 그리고 그는 그 한쪽 끝을 자신의 벨트 뒤에 묶었고 반대쪽 끝을 자신의 엄마에게 주었습니다.

"저를 내려주세요." 그가 말했습니다. "그럼 제가 반지를 찾아볼게요."

"고맙구나, 스탠리." 램찹 부인이 말했습니다. 그녀는 그를 창살 사이로 내려주었고 조심스럽게 위아래 그리고 이쪽저쪽으로 그를 움직여서, 그가 통로의 모든 바닥을 찾아볼 수 있게 했습니다.

두 경찰이 다가와서 램찹 부인을 빤히 쳐다보았을 때 그녀는 격자 뚜껑을 지나 아래로 내려가는 긴 끈을 들고 서 있었습니다. 그녀는 그들을 보지 못한 척 했습니다.

"무슨 일이신가요, 부인?" 첫 번째 경찰관이 물었습니다. "당신의 요요가 걸렸나요?"

"난 요요를 갖고 장난치는 게 아니에요!" 램찹 부인이 날카롭게 말했습니다. "제 아들이 이 끈의 반대쪽 끝에 있어요, 당신들이 정 그렇게 알고 싶다면 말이에요."

"그물을 가져와, 해리(Harry)." 두 번째 경찰관이 말했습니다. "우리는 미친 사람을 잡은 것 같아!"

바로 그때, 통로 아래에서, 스탠리가 외쳤습니다. "만세!"

램찹 부인은 그를 끌어 올렸고 그가 반지를 가진 것을 보았습니다.

"잘했어, 스탠리." 그녀가 말했습니다. 그리고는 그녀는 화를 내며 경찰에게 돌아섰습니다.

"미친 사람이지요, 정말로!" 그녀가 말했습니다. "부끄러운 줄 알아요!"

경찰은 사과했습니다. "우리는 이해하지 못했어요, 부인." 그들이 말했습니다. "우리가 경솔했네요. 우리가 그랬다는 걸 이제 알겠어요."

"사람들은 무례한 발언을 하기 전에 신중하게 생각해야 해요." 램찹 부인이 말했습니다. "그다음에는 그런 말을 아예 하지 말아야죠."

경찰은 그것이 좋은 규칙이라는 것을 깨달았고 자신들이 그것을 기억하겠다고 말했습니다.

어느 날 스탠리는 가족이 최근에 캘리포니아로 이사 간, 자기 친구 토마스 앤서니 제프리(Thomas Anthony Jeffrey)에게서 편지를 받았습니다. 학교 방학이 시작될 참이었고, 스탠리는 제프리 가족과 함께 지내자고 초대를 받았습니다.

"오, 이런!" 스탠리가 말했습니다. "난 정말 가고 싶어!"

램찹 씨는 한숨을 쉬었습니다. "캘리포니아로 가는 기차나 비행기 왕복표는 몹시 비싸단다." 그가 말했습니다. "난 더 저렴한 방법을 생각해내야만 하겠구나."

램찹 씨가 그날 저녁에 사무실에서 집으로 왔을 때, 그는 커다란 갈색 종이 봉투를 들고 왔습니다.

"자 이제, 스탠리." 그가 말했습니다. "이게 맞는지 입어보렴."

그 봉투는 스탠리에게 매우 잘 맞았습니다. 램찹 부인이 발견하기로는, 심지어 거기에는 얇은 빵으로 만든 달걀 샐러드 샌드위치, 그리고 우유를 채운 칫솔 통을 넣을 수 있는 남는 공간도 있었습니다.

그들은 항공 우편과 보험 비용을 내기 위해 봉투에 정말로 많은 우표를 붙여야 했지만, 여전히 캘리포니아로 가는 기차나 비행기 표보다는 훨씬 덜 비쌌습니다.

다음 날 램찹 부부는 스탠리를 달걀 샐러드 샌드위치와 우유가 가득 담긴 칫솔 통과 함께 그의 봉투 속으로 밀어 넣었고, 모퉁이에 있는 우편함을 통해 그를 부쳤습니다. 봉투를 구멍으로 넣으려면 접어야만 했지만, 스탠리는 유연한 남자아이였고, 우편함 안에서 그는 다시 몸을 바르게 펼 수 있었습니다.

스탠리가 이전에 혼자서 집을 떠난 적이 한 번도 없었기 때문에 램찹 부인은 걱정스러웠습니다. 그녀는 우편함을 쾅쾅 두드렸습니다.

"엄마 말 들리니, 얘야?" 그녀가 불렀습니다. "너 다 괜찮니?"

스탠리의 목소리가 꽤 분명하게 들렸습니다. "전 괜찮아요. 저 지금 제 샌드위치 먹어도 돼요?"

"한 시간은 기다려. 그리고 너무 뜨거워지지 않도록 하렴, 얘야." 램찹 부인이 말했습니다. 그리고는 그녀와 램찹 씨가 외쳤습니다. "안녕, 잘 다녀와!" 그리고는 집으로 갔습니다.

스탠리는 캘리포니아에서 좋은 시간을 보냈습니다. 그 방문이 끝났을 때, 제프리 가족은 자신들이 직접 만든 아름다운 흰색 봉투 안에 그를 담아 돌려보냈습니다. 그것에는 붉고 파란 표시가 있어 그것이 항공우편이라는 것을 나타

내주었고, 토마스 제프리는 "귀중품" 그리고 "취급 주의" 또 "이쪽이 위로 가게 놓으시오"라고 그것의 양면에 적어 놓았습니다.

집으로 돌아와서 스탠리는 자신의 가족에게 그가 정말로 조심스럽게 다루어져서 단 한 번도 부딪히는 것을 느껴보지 못했다고 말했습니다. 램찹 씨는 그것이 제트기가 훌륭하고, 우편 서비스도 마찬가지로 훌륭하며, 이는 살기에 아주 좋은 시대임을 증명하는 것이라고 말했습니다.

스탠리 또한, 그렇게 생각했습니다.

3장 연이 된 스탠리

램찹 씨는 일요일 오후에 아이들을 박물관이나 공원에 있는 롤러스케이트장으로 데리고 나가는 것을 언제나 좋아했지만, 그들이 길을 건너거나 많은 사람 사이에서 이동하는 것은 힘이 들었습니다. 스탠리와 아서는 종종 그의 옆에서 거칠게 밀쳐졌고 램찹 씨는 과속하는 택시나 급히 이동하는 사람들이 혹시라도 그들을 쳐서 넘어뜨릴까 봐 걱정했습니다.

스탠리가 납작해진 후에는 더 수월해졌습니다.

램찹 씨는 자신이 스탠리를 전혀 다치

게 하지 않고서 그를 돌돌 말 수 있다는 것을 알아차렸습니다. 그는 스탠리의 몸에 한 가닥의 줄을 묶어 그가 펼쳐지는 것을 막기도 하고 그 줄로 그가 잡을 작은 고리를 만들었습니다. 그건 소포를 운반하는 것만큼이나 간단했고, 그는 다른 손으로 아서를 잡을 수 있었습니다.

스탠리는 들려서 가는 것을 전혀 신경 쓰지 않았는데 왜냐하면 그는 걷는 것을 그다지 좋아하지 않았기 때문입니다. 아서 역시 걷는 것을 좋아하지 않았지만, 그는 그래야만 했지요. 그건 그를 화나게 했습니다.

어느 일요일 오후, 길에서, 그들은 램찹 씨의 오래된 대학 친구인 랠프 존스(Ralph Jones)를 만났습니다.

"흠, 조지, 내가 보기엔 네가 벽지를 좀 산 것 같은데." 존스 씨가 말했습니다. "자네 집을 꾸미려는 거겠지?"

"벽지라니?" 램찹 씨가 말했습니다. "오, 아니야. 이건 내 아들 스탠리야."

그는 끈을 풀었고 스탠리가 펼쳐졌습니다.

"안녕하세요?" 스탠리가 말했습니다.

"만나서 반갑구나, 어린 친구." 존스 씨가 말했습니다. "조지." 그가 램찹 씨에게 말했습니다. "저 아이는 납작하잖아."

"또한, 똑똑하기도 하지." 램찹 씨가 말했습니다. "학교에서 스탠리는 자기 반에서 3등이야."

"쳇!" 아서가 말했습니다.

"여기는 내 막내아들 아서라네." 램찹 씨가 말했습니다. "그리고 이 녀석은 자신의 무례함에 대해서 사과할 거야."

아서는 얼굴을 붉히며 사과를 할 수밖에 없었습니다.

램찹 씨는 다시 스탠리를 돌돌 말았고 그들은 집으로 향했습니다. 그들이 가는 동안에 비가 꽤 많이 내렸습니다. 스탠리는, 물론, 끝에만 젖었을 뿐, 거의 전혀 젖지 않았지만, 아서는 흠뻑 젖고 말았습니다.

그날 밤 늦게 램찹 부부는 거실에서 나는 소음을 들었습니다. 그들은 아서가 책장 옆 바닥에 누워있는 것을 발견했습니다. 그는 자신의 몸 위에 많은 권수의 브리태니커 백과사전(Encyclopaedia Britannica) 책들을 쌓아놓았습니다.

"몇 권 더 제 몸 위로 올려주세요." 아서가 그들을 보았을 때 그가 말했습니다. "그냥 거기에 그렇게 서 있지 말고요. 절 도와주세요."

램찹 부부는 그를 다시 잠자리로 돌려보냈고, 다음 날 아침에 스탠리에게 말했습니다. "아서가 질투하는 것도 당연하단다." 그들이 말했습니다. "그에게 잘해주렴. 어쨌거나, 넌 그의 형이잖니."

그 다음 일요일에, 스탠리와 아서는 둘이서만 공원에 갔습니다. 그날은 화창했지만, 바람이 불기도 했고, 많은 더 나이 많은 남자아이들이 긴 꼬리가 달리고, 온갖 무지개 색으로 만들어진 아름답고, 커다란 연을 날리고 있었습니다.

아서가 한숨 쉬었습니다. "언젠가는 말이야." 그가 말했습니다. "나는 큰 연을 가질 거야, 그리고 나는 연날리기 대회에서 이겨서 다른 모든 사람처럼 유명해지고 말 거야. 요즘에는 아무도 내가 누구인지 몰라."

스탠리는 자신의 부모님이 뭐라고 말씀하셨는지 기억했습니다. 그는 연이 고장 난 남자아이에게 가서 큰 실패를 빌렸습니다.

"넌 나를 날리면 돼, 아서." 그가 말했습니다. "해 봐."

그는 자신의 몸에 끈을 묶었고 아서에게 실패를 주어 잡게 했습니다. 그는 가볍게 잔디를 가로지르며, 속력을 내기 위해 옆으로 달렸고, 그리고 그는 바람을 맞기 위해 돌아섰습니다.

위로, 위로, 위로. . .위로! 스탠리가 연이 되어, 올라갔습니다.

그는 불어오는 강한 바람을 어떻게 다루어야 할지 정확히 알고 있었습니다. 그는 자신이 올라가고 싶으면, 바람을 정면으로 마주 보았고, 그가 속도를 내고 싶을 때는 바람이 그를 뒤에서 밀도록 했습니다. 그는 때때로 약간씩, 자기 몸의 얇은 가장자리 면을 바람을 향해, 조심스럽게, 돌려주기만 하면 되었는데, 그러면 바람이 그를 붙들지 못했고, 그리고는 그는 우아하게 땅으로 다시 미끄러지듯 내려올 수 있었습니다.

아서는 모든 끈을 풀었고, 그의 빨간 셔츠와 파란 바지를 입은 모습이 옅은 푸른 하늘과 대비되어 아름다운 광경을 만들며, 스탠리는 나무들 위로 높이 솟구쳤습니다.

공원에 있는 모든 사람이 가만히 서서 지켜보았습니다.

스탠리는 오른쪽으로 급강하하더니 그다음에는 왼쪽으로 길고, 비슷한 급강하를 했습니다. 그는 자기 양옆으로 자신의 팔을 뻗고서 로켓처럼 쌩 하고 빠르게 땅으로 다가왔고 다시 곡선으로 그리며 태양을 향해 올라갔습니다. 그는 옆으로 회전했다가 다시 수평으로 비행하고 빙글빙글 돌았고, 숫자 8, 십자가, 그리고 별 모양을 그렸습니다.

누구도 그날 스탠리 램찹이 날았던 방식으로 날았던 적이 없었습니다. 아마도 누구도 다시 그러지 못할 테지요.

얼마 후에는, 당연하게도, 사람들은 구경하는 것에 질렸고, 아서는 빈 실패를 들고 이리저리 뛰어다니는 것에 지쳤습니다. 그렇지만, 스탠리는 계속 그러고 있었지요. 뽐내는 것을 말이에요.

세 소년이 아서에게 다가왔고 그들이 핫도그와 탄산음료를 먹으러 가는 데 그를 초대했습니다. 아서는 갈라진 나무 사이에 실패를 끼워 두었습니다. 그는 눈치 채지 못했는데, 그가 핫도그를 먹는 동안에, 바람이 끈을 날려서 나무에 엉기게 했다는 것을 말입니다.

끈은 점점 더 짧아졌지만, 스탠리는 자신의 발에 잎들이 닿기 전까지는 자기가 얼마나 낮게 나는지 깨닫지 못했고, 너무 늦고 말았습니다. 그는 나뭇가지에 걸렸습니다. 15분이 지나고 나서야 아서와 다른 남자아이들이 그의 울음을 듣고 올라가서 그를 풀어 주었습니다.

스탠리는 그날 저녁, 그리고 잠자리에 들 때도 그의 동생과 말을 하지 않았는데, 비록 아서가 사과하기 했지만, 그는 여전히 뚱해 있었습니다.

램찹 씨와 거실에 단둘이 남자, 램찹 부인은 한숨 쉬며 자신의 고개를 저었습니다. "당신은 온종일 사무실에 있으면서, 즐겁게 시간을 보냈겠지요." 그녀가 말했습니다. "당신은 내가 아이들이랑 무슨 일을 겪어야 했는지 알지 못할 거예요. 애들이 몹시 까다롭게 굴었어요."

"애들이 다 그런 거죠." 램찹 씨가 말했습니다. "그럴 시기예요. 인내심을 가져요, 여보."

4장 미술관 도둑

오. 제이 다트 부부(Mr. and Mrs. O. Jay Dart)는 램찹 가족 위에 있는 아파트에 살았습니다. 다트 씨는 중요한 사람으로서, 시내 중심가에 있는 유명한 미술관(Famous Museum of Art)의 관장이었습니다.

스탠리 램찹은 엘리베이터 안에서 평소에는 활기찬 사람인 다트 씨가, 상당히 우울해하고 있다는 것을 알아차렸지만, 그는 이유가 무엇인지 알지 못했습니다. 그리고 어느 아침에 아침 식사를 하다가 그는 램찹 부부가 다트 씨에 대해서 이야기하는 것을 들었습니다.

"내가 읽기로는." 램찹 씨가 자신의 커피 컵 너머로 신문을 읽으면서, 말했습니다. "유명한 미술관에서 또 그림을 도둑맞았다고 하네. 여기 기사에서는 관장인 오. 제이 다트 씨가 좋은 수가 없어 어쩌지 못한다고 말하고 있어요."

"오, 이런! 경찰은 아무 도움이 되지 않는데요?" 램찹 부인이 물었습니다.

"그런 것 같지 않아요." 램찹 씨가 말했습니다. "경찰 서장이 언론에 뭐라고 말했는지 들어 봐요. '우리는 좀도둑 일당을 의심하고 있습니다. 이들이 가장

악질적인 종류이지요. 그들은 은밀하게 활동해서, 그들을 잡는 것을 매우 어렵게 하고 있습니다. 하지만, 제 부하들과 저는 계속 노력할 것입니다. 한편, 저는 사람들이 경찰 댄스파티의 입장권을 사고 그들의 차량을 주차금지 표지판이 있는 곳에 주차하지 않기를 바랍니다.'"

다음 날 아침 스탠리 램찹은 다트 씨가 엘리베이터 안에서 그의 아내에게 말하는 것을 들었습니다.

"이 좀도둑들은 밤에 활동해요." 다트 씨가 말했습니다. "우리 경비원들이 낮에 종일 근무를 선 다음에 깨어 있는 것은 상당히 어려운 일이에요. 그리고 유명한 미술관은 무척 커서, 우리는 모든 그림을 동시에 지킬 수는 없어요. 난 그게 가망 없고, 절망적이고, 희망이 없는 상황일까 봐 두려워요!"

문득, 마치 그의 머리 위 허공에서 전기 전구가 켜진 것처럼, 약간 흥분된 기색을 내뿜으며, 스탠리 램찹에게 좋은 생각이 떠올랐습니다. 그는 그것을 다트 씨에게 말했습니다.

"스탠리." 다트 씨가 말했습니다. "만약에 네 어머니가 허락해 주신다면, 난 오늘 밤 당장 네가 네 계획을 실행에 옮기도록 할 거란다!"

램찹 부인은 허락했습니다. "하지만 넌 오늘 오후에 긴 낮잠을 자야만 하겠구나." 그녀가 말했습니다. "난 네가 일어나야만 하지 않는다면 늦게까지 너를 깨우지 않을게."

그날 저녁, 긴 낮잠을 자고 나서, 스탠리는 다트 씨와 함께 유명한 미술관에 갔습니다. 다트 씨는 그를 본관으로 데리고 갔는데, 그곳에는 가장 크고 가장 중요한 그림들이 걸려 있었습니다. 그는 턱수염이 난 남자가 축 처진 벨벳 모자를 쓴 채, 긴 의자 위에 누운 여인을 위해 바이올린을 연주하는 모습을 보여주는 큰 그림을 가리켰습니다. 거기에는 반은 인간, 반은 말의 모습을 한 사람이 그들 뒤에 서 있었고, 날개가 달린 뚱뚱한 아이들 세 명이 위에서 날아다니고 있었습니다. 저 그림은, 다트 씨가 설명하기로는, 이 세상에서 가장 비싼 그림이었습니다.

반대편 벽에는 빈 액자가 있었습니다. 우리는 그것에 대해서 나중에 더 듣게 될 것입니다.

다트 씨는 스탠리를 그의 사무실 안으로 데려갔고 말했습니다. "이제 네가 변장을 할 시간이란다."

"전 이미 그것에 대해 생각해 뒀어요." 스탠리 램찹이 말했습니다. "그리고 전 변장할 것을 가져왔지요. 제 카우보이 복장이에요. 거기엔 빨간 반다나(bandanna)가 있어서 제가 제 얼굴 위로 묶을 수 있어요. 백만 년 안에는 아무도 저를 알아보지 못할 거에요."

"안 돼." 다트 씨가 말했습니다. "너는 내가 고른 변장을 입어야만 한단다."

옷장에서 그는 파란 장식 끈이 달린 하얀 드레스, 반짝거리는 작은 뾰족구두 한 켤레, 장식 끈과 색이 맞는 파란 띠가 달린 넓은 밀짚모자, 그리고 가발과 막대기를 꺼냈습니다. 가발은 금발로 이루어졌고, 곱슬머리였습니다. 막대기는 윗부분이 구부러졌고 그것에도 또한, 파란 리본이 달려 있었습니다.

"이 양치기 소녀 변장이라면." 다트 씨가 말했습니다. "넌 본관에 어울리는 그림처럼 보일 거야. 우리는 본관에 카우보이 그림을 두지 않는단다."

스탠리는 너무 혐오스러워서, 거의 말을 할 수가 없었습니다. "전 여자애처럼 보일 거고, 그게 바로 제가 보여지게 될 모습이에요." 그가 말했습니다. "제가 아이디어를 아예 떠올리지 않았더라면 좋았겠어요."

하지만 그는 너그러운 사람이었기에, 그 변장을 했습니다.

다시 본관으로 돌아와서, 다트 씨는 스탠리가 그 빈 액자 안으로 올라가는 것을 도와주었습니다. 스탠리는 제자리에 고정되어 있을 수 있었는데 왜냐하면 다트 씨가 현명하게도, 각각 손과 발에 하나씩, 네 개의 작은 쇠못을 벽에 박아 두었기 때문입니다.

액자는 완벽하게 맞았습니다. 벽에 걸리자, 스탠리는 꼭 마치 그림처럼 보였습니다.

"단지 하나만 제외하고 말이야." 다트 씨가 말했습니다. "양치기 소녀는 행복하게 보여야만 해. 그들은 자신들의 양과 하늘을 향해 미소 짓는다고. 너는 험악해 보이잖니, 행복한 게 아니라, 스탠리."

스탠리는 자신의 두 눈에 멍하니 꿈꾸는 듯한 기색을 담으려고 열심히 노력했고 심지어 조금이라도 미소 지으려고 했습니다.

다트 씨는 몇 걸음 뒤로 물러났고 잠시 그를 쳐다보았습니다. "뭐." 그가 말했습니다. "그건 예술은 아닐지도 모르지, 하지만 난 내가 무엇을 좋아하는지 아니까."

그는 스탠리의 계획 가운데 어떤 다른 부분이 처리되었는지 확인하려고 떠났고, 스탠리는 혼자 남겨졌습니다.

본관은 무척 어두웠습니다. 약간의 달빛이 창문 사이로 들어왔고, 스탠리는 단지 반대편 벽에 있는 세상에서 가장 비싼 그림만을 알아볼 수 있었습니다. 그는 바이올린을 든 턱수염이 난 남자와 긴 의자 위에 있는 여자와 반은 말의 모습을 한 인간과 날개가 달린 아이들이 모두, 그와 마찬가지로, 무슨 일이 일어나기를 기다리는 것 같다고 느꼈습니다.

시간이 흘렀고 그는 점점 더 지쳐갔습니다. 누구라도 이렇게 늦은 밤이라면 피곤할 것입니다. 특히 작은 쇠못 위에서 중심을 잡은 채 액자 안에 서 있어야만 한다면 말이에요.

아마도 그들이 오지 않을지도 몰라, 스탠리는 생각했습니다. 아마도 좀도둑이 아예 오지 않을 수도 있어.

달이 구름 뒤로 숨자 본관은 칠흑같이 어두워졌습니다. 또한, 그 어두움으로 인해, 더 고요해진 듯했습니다. 전혀 아무 소리도 나지 않았습니다. 스탠리는 그의 목 뒤에 난 머리칼이 가발의 구불거리는 머리카락 아래에서 곤두서는 게 느껴졌습니다.

삐-이이이-이이이-걱. . .

삐걱거리는 소리가 본관의 바로 중앙에서 들려왔고, 심지어 그가 그 소리를 들었을 때, 스탠리는 보았습니다, 같은 곳에서 나오는, 아주 작은 은은한 노란 불빛을 말이죠!

삐걱거리는 소리가 다시 났고, 은은한 불빛이 더 커졌습니다. 바닥에서 작은 문이 열렸고, 두 남자가 그것을 통해서 전시실로 올라왔습니다!

스탠리는 한 번에 모든 것을 이해했습니다. 이들이 그 좀도둑인 게 분명했습니다! 그들이 바깥에서 미술관 안으로 들어갈 수 있는 입구로 비밀 작은 문을 만들어 둔 것입니다. 그게 바로 그들이 한 번도 잡히지 않은 이유였습니다. 그리고 이제, 오늘 밤, 그들은 세상에서 가장 비싼 그림을 훔치기 위해 돌아왔습니다!

그는 자신의 액자 안에서 아주 가만히 있었고 좀도둑이 하는 말을 들었습니다.

"바로 이거야, 맥스(Max)" 첫 번째 남자가 말했습니다. "여기가 바로 우리 예술품 절도범들이 문명사회가 잠든 사이에 세상을 놀라게 할 일을 벌일 장소라고."

"맞아, 루터(Luther)." 다른 남자가 말했습니다. "이 큰 도시 전체에서, 우리를 의심할 사람은 아무도 없어."

하, 하! 스탠리 램찹이 생각했습니다. 그건 당신들 생각이고!

좀도둑은 자신들의 손전등을 내려놓고 세상에서 가장 비싼 그림을 벽에서 떼어 냈습니다.

"우리를 잡으려고 하는 사람에게 우리가 어떻게 해야 할까, 맥스?" 첫 번째 남자가 물었습니다.

"우리는 그 사람을 죽일 거야. 달리 뭘 더 하겠어?" 그의 친구가 대답했습니다.

그건 스탠리를 두렵게 하는 데 충분했고, 루터가 다가와서 그를 빤히 쳐다보자 그는 훨씬 더 겁이 났습니다.

"이 양치기 소녀 말이야." 루터가 말했

습니다. "난 양치기 소녀는 원래 미소 지어야 한다고 생각했는데, 맥스. 이 소녀는 두려워하는 것처럼 보여."

때맞춰, 스탠리는 가까스로 멍하니 꿈꾸는 듯한 기색을 그의 두 눈에 다시 담았고 미소, 비슷한 것을 지을 수 있었습니다.

"너 정신 나갔구나, 루터." 맥스가 말했습니다. "그녀가 미소 짓고 있잖아. 그리고 또, 그녀는 정말 어여쁜 소녀이기도 해."

그 말이 스탠리를 분노하게 했습니다. 그는 좀도둑들이 다시 세상에서 가장 비싼 그림을 향해 돌아설 때까지 기다렸고, 그는 자신이 낼 수 있는 가장 크고, 가장 무시무시한 목소리로 외쳤습니다: **"경찰! 경찰 아저씨! 다트 씨! 좀도둑들이 여기 있어요!"**

좀도둑들이 서로를 바라보았습니다. "맥스." 첫 번째 남자가 아주 조용하게 말했습니다. "내가 양치기 소녀가 소리 지르는 것을 들은 것 같아."

"나도 그렇게 생각해." 맥스가 떨리는 목소리로 말했습니다. "오, 맙소사! 소리 지르는 그림이라니. 우리 둘 다 휴식이 필요해."

"너희는 휴식을 취하게 되겠지(get a rest), 그렇고말고!" 다트 씨가 외치면서, 자신의 뒤로 경찰 서장과 많은 경비원 그리고 경찰들을 데리고 황급히 달려왔습니다. "너희는 *체포될 거야.(get ar-rested)*, 그게 너희 운명이지! 하, 하, 하!"

좀도둑은 다트 씨의 농담에 너무 혼란스러웠고 경찰들 때문에 너무 겁을 먹어서 싸움을 일으키지도 못했습니다.

그들이 미처 알아차리기 전에, 그들은 수갑이 채워졌고 교도소로 이송되었습니다.

다음 날 아침 경찰 서장의 사무실에서, 스탠리 램찹이 메달을 받았습니다. 그 바로 다음 날에는 그의 사진이 모든 신문에 실렸습니다.

5장 아서의 좋은 생각

한동안 스탠리 램찹은 유명한 이름이었습니다. 스탠리가 가는 모든 곳에서, 사람들이 쳐다보았고 그를 가리켰습니다. 그는 그들이 속삭이는 것을 들을 수 있었습니다. "저기야, 아그네스(Agnes), 저기 말이야! 저 사람이 분명히 스탠리 램찹일 거야, 그 좀도둑들을 잡은 사람 있잖아. . ." 그리고 그것과 비슷한 말들을 말이에요.

하지만 몇 주가 지나자 속삭이는 것과 쳐다보는 것이 멈췄습니다. 사람들에게는 생각해야 할 다른 일들이 있었지요. 스탠리는 신경 쓰지 않았어요. 유명해진다는 것은 재미있었지만, 그것으로 충분했습니다.

그러고 나서 또 다른 변화가 생겼는데, 그것은 유쾌한 일은 아니었습니다. 사람들은 그가 지나갈 때 그를 비웃고 놀리기 시작했습니다. "안녕, 삐쩍 마른 아이(Super-Skinny)!" 그들은 이렇게 소리치곤 했지요. 그리고 그의 외모에 대해서 훨씬 더 무례한 말들도 했습니다.

스탠리는 자신의 부모님에게 그가 어떻게 느끼는지 말했습니다. "제가 주로 신경 쓰이는 건 다른 아이들이에요." 그가 말했습니다. "그들은 더는 저를 좋아하지 않아요. 왜냐하면 제가 다르기 때문이에요. 납작하니까요."

"그들이 부끄러운 짓을 하는 거란다." 램찹 부인이 말했습니다. "사람들의 체형을 가지고 그들을 싫어하는 건 잘못된 거야. 그 점에 있어서, 그들의 종교나 혹은 그들의 피부색 때문에 말이야."

"저도 알아요." 스탠리가 말했습니다. "단지 아마도 모든 사람이 모두를 좋아하는 건 불가능한가 봐요."

"아마 그럴지도 모르지." 램찹 부인이 말했습니다. "하지만 사람들은 노력할 수 있단다."

그날 밤에 아서 램찹은 우는 소리에 잠에서 깼습니다. 어둠 속에서 그는 방을 가로질러 살금살금 걸어가 스탠리의 침대 옆에 무릎을 꿇고 앉았습니다.

"형 괜찮아?" 그가 말했습니다.

"저리 가." 스탠리가 말했습니다.

"나한테 화내지 마." 아서가 말했습니다. "형이 내 연이었을 때 내가 형을 걸리게 내버려 둬서 형이 아직도 화가 난 것 같네, 내가 보기엔."

"그냥 넘어가, 응?" 스탠리가 말했습니다. "난 화가 난 게 아니야. 저리 가라고."

"제발 사이 좋게 지내자. . . ." 아서도 또한, 약간 울지 않을 수 없었습니다. "오, 스탠리 형." 그가 말했습니다. "제발 나한테 뭐가 문제인지 말해 줘."

스탠리는 오랜 시간을 기다린 후에 말을 했습니다. "문제는 있지." 그가 말했습니다. "나는 그저 더는 행복하지 않아. 나는 납작한 상태로 있는 데 질렸어. 나는 다시 평범한 형태로 돌아가고 싶어, 다른 사람처럼 말이야. 하지만 나는 평생 납작해진 채로 계속 있어야만 할 거야. 그게 나를 지긋지긋하게 해."

"오, 스탠리 형." 아서가 말했습니다. 그는 자기 눈물을 스탠리의 침대 시트 끝으로 닦았고 뭐라고 더 말해야 할지 떠올리지 못했습니다.

"내가 방금 한 말에 대해서 말하고 다니지 마." 스탠리가 그에게 말했습니다. "나는 부모님이 걱정하시는 걸 바라지 않아. 그건 단지 상황을 악화시킬 뿐이야."

"형은 용감해." 아서가 말했습니다. "정말이야."

그는 스탠리의 손을 잡았습니다. 두 형제는 어둠 속에서 함께 앉아서, 친구가 되었습니다. 그들은 둘 다 슬펐지만, 각자 그 전에 느꼈던 것보다는 조금 기분이 나아졌습니다.

그때, 갑자기, 그가 심지어 생각해 내려고 노력하지도 않았는데도 불구하고, 아서에게 좋은 생각이 났습니다. 그는 벌떡 일어나서 불을 켰고 장난감과 물건을 담은 큰 보관함으로 달려갔습니다. 그는 상자를 뒤지기 시작했습니다.

스탠리는 침대에 앉아서 지켜보았습니다.

아서는 축구공과 장난감 병정 몇 개 그리고 비행기 모형과 많은 나무 장난감 블록들을 옆으로 휙 던졌고, 그러더니 그가 말했습니다. "아하!" 그가 자신이 원하던 것을 찾았습니다—바로 낡은 자전거 공기 주입 펌프였습니다. 그는 그것을 들어 올렸고, 스탠리와 그는 서로를 바라보았습니다.

"좋아." 스탠리가 마침내 말했습니다. "하지만 조심해." 그는 긴 펌프 호스의 끝을 자기 입에 넣었고 자신의 입술로 그 주변을 꾹 다물어서 공기가 빠져나가지 않게 했습니다.

"내가 천천히 할게." 아서가 말했습니다. "혹시 그게 아프거나 그러면, 나한테 형의 손을 흔들어."

그러더니 그는 공기를 넣기 시작했습니다. 처음에는 스탠리의 뺨이 약간 부풀어 오르는 것 외에 아무 일도 일어나지 않았습니다. 아서는 형의 손을 지켜보았지만, 그 어떤 꿈틀거리는 신호도 없어서, 그는 계속 펌프질했습니다. 그때, 갑자기, 스탠리의 상체가 부풀기 시작했습니다.

"그게 효과가 있어! 효과가 있다고!" 아서가 펌프질을 하면서, 외쳤습니다.

스탠리는 자신의 팔을 뻗어서 공기가 자신의 몸 안에서 더 수월하게 이동하도록 했습니다. 그는 점점 더 커졌습니다. 그의 잠옷 상의에 달린 단추들이 터져 나갔습니다—펑! 펑! 펑! 잠시 후에 그는 모두 부풀어 올랐습니다; 머리와 몸, 팔과 다리까지 말이지요. 하지만 그의 오른발은 아니었어요. 그 발은 납작해진 상태로 남아있었습니다.

아서는 펌프질하는 것을 멈췄습니다. "그건 마치 그 긴 풍선들의 마지막 남은 부분을 불려고 하는 것과 같아." 그가 말했습니다. "아마도 흔드는 것이 도움이 될 거야."

스탠리는 자신의 오른발을 두 번 흔들었고, 작은 쉭 하는 소리가 나면서 그것이 왼발과 마찬가지로 부풀어 올랐습니다. 마치 그가 결코 납작해졌던 적이 없다는 듯이, 예전에 그랬던 모습 그대로 스탠리 램찹이 그곳에 서 있었습니다.

"고마워, 아서." 스탠리가 말했습니다. "정말로 고마워."

형제가 악수하고 있었을 때 램찹 씨가 바로 그의 뒤를 따라오는 램찹 부인과 함께 방으로 성큼성큼 들어왔습니다. "우리가 너희가 내는 소리를 들었어!" 램찹 씨가 말했습니다. "너희가 자야만 하는 시간에 일어나서 떠들다니, 응? 부끄러운 줄—"

"**조지!**" 램찹 부인이 말했습니다. "스탠리가 다시 둥그렇게 됐어요!"

"당신 말이 맞아요!" 램찹 씨가 알아채며, 말했습니다. "잘 됐구나, 스탠리!"

"제가 그렇게 해 줬어요." 아서가 말했습니다. "제가 그에게 바람을 넣어 줬어요."

물론, 모두 몹시 흥분하고 행복해했습니다. 램찹 부인은 코코아를 만들어 이 일을 축하했고, 아서의 재치를 기리며 그를 위해 여러 차례 건배하며 마셨습니다.

이 작은 파티가 끝나자, 램찹 부부는 다시 아이들을 그들의 침대에 눕혔고 그들에게 뽀뽀해 준 다음, 그들은 불을 껐습니다. "잘 자렴." 그들이 말했습니다.

"안녕히 주무세요." 스탠리와 아서가 말했습니다.

길고 피곤한 하루였습니다. 얼마 지나지 않아 모든 램찹 가족들은 잠이 들었습니다.

끝

Chapter 1

1. C "Hey! Come and look! Hey!" Mr. and Mrs. Lambchop were both very much in favor of politeness and careful speech. "Hay is for horses, Arthur, not people," Mr. Lambchop said as they entered the bedroom.

2. A Across it lay the enormous bulletin board that Mr. Lambchop had given the boys a Christmas ago so that they could pin up pictures and messages and maps.

3. D It had fallen, during the night, on top of Stanley.

4. C "Let's all have breakfast," Mrs. Lambchop said. "Then Stanley and I will go see Dr. Dan and hear what he has to say."

5. C Mrs. Lambchop said she thought Stanley's clothes would have to be altered by the tailor now, so Dr. Dan told his nurse to take Stanley's measurements.

Chapter 2

1. A When Stanley got used to being flat, he enjoyed it. He could go in and out of rooms, even when the door was closed, just by lying down and sliding through the crack at the bottom.

2. D "Lower me," he said, "and I will look for the ring." "Thank you, Stanley," Mrs. Lambchop said. She lowered him between the bars and moved him carefully up and down and from side to side, so that he could search the whole floor of the shaft.

3. C Two policemen came by and stared at Mrs. Lambchop as she stood holding the long lace that ran down through the grating. She pretended not to notice them. "What's the matter, lady?" the first policeman asked. "Is your yo-yo stuck?" "I am not playing with a yo-yo!" Mrs. Lambchop said sharply. "My son is at the other end of this lace, if you must know." "Get the net, Harry," said the second policeman. "We have caught a cuckoo!"

4. B Mr. Lambchop sighed. "A round-trip train or airplane ticket to California is very expensive," he said. "I will have to think of some cheaper way." When

Mr. Lambchop came home from the office that evening, he brought with him an enormous brown-paper envelope. "Now then, Stanley," he said. "Try this for size."

5. D Back home Stanley told his family that he had been handled so carefully he never felt a single bump.

Chapter 3

1. B Mr. Lambchop had always liked to take the boys out with him on Sunday afternoons, to a museum or roller-skating in the park, but it was difficult when they were crossing streets or moving about in crowds. Stanley and Arthur would often be jostled from his side and Mr. Lambchop worried about speeding taxis or that hurrying people might accidentally knock them down. It was easier after Stanley got flat. Mr. Lambchop discovered that he could roll Stanley up without hurting him at all.

2. C Late that night Mr. and Mrs. Lambchop heard a noise out in the living room. They found Arthur lying on the floor near the bookcase. He had piled a great many volumes of the *Encyclopaedia Britannica* on top of himself. "Put some more on me," Arthur said when he saw them. "Don't just stand there. Help me." Mr. and Mrs. Lambchop sent him back to bed, but the next morning they spoke to Stanley. "Arthur can't help being jealous," they said.

3. A Arthur sighed. "Someday," he said, "I will have a big kite, and I will win a kite-flying contest and be famous like everyone else. *Nobody* knows who I am these days." Stanley remembered what his parents had said. He went to a boy whose kite was broken and borrowed a large spool of string. "You can fly me, Arthur," he said. "Come on."

4. C Arthur left the spool wedged in the fork of a tree. He did not notice, while he was eating the hot dog, that the wind was blowing the string and tangling it about the tree. The string got shorter and shorter, but Stanley did not realize how low he was until leaves brushed his feet, and then it was too late. He got stuck in the branches.

5. D Stanley would not speak to his brother that evening, and at bedtime, even though Arthur had apologized, he was still cross.

Chapter 4

1. C Stanley Lambchop had noticed in the elevator that Mr. Dart, who was ordinarily a cheerful man, had become quite gloomy, but he had no idea what the reason was. And then at breakfast one morning he heard Mr. and Mrs. Lambchop talking about Mr. Dart. "I see," said Mr. Lambchop, reading the paper over his coffee cup, "that still another painting has been stolen from the Famous Museum. It says here that Mr. O. Jay Dart, the director, is at his wits' end."

2. A The next morning Stanley Lambchop heard Mr. Dart talking to his wife in the elevator. "These sneak thieves work at night," Mr. Dart said. "It is very hard for our guards to stay awake when they have been on duty all day. And the Famous Museum is so big, we cannot guard every picture at the same time."

3. D "In this shepherdess disguise," Mr. Dart said, "you will look like a painting that belongs in the main hall. We do not have cowboy pictures in the main hall."

4. B A trapdoor had opened in the floor, and two men came up through it into the hall! Stanley understood everything all at once. These must be the sneak thieves! They had a secret trapdoor entrance into the museum from outside. That was why they had never been caught.

5. B He waited until the sneak thieves had turned back to the world's most expensive painting, and he shouted in his loudest, most terrifying voice: "POLICE! POLICE! MR. DART! THE SNEAK THIEVES ARE HERE!"

Chapter 5

1. B And then came a further change, and it was not a pleasant one. People began to laugh and make fun of him as he passed by. "Hello, Super-Skinny!"

they would shout, and even ruder things, about the way he looked. Stanley told his parents how he felt. "It's the other kids I mostly mind," he said. "They don't like me anymore because I'm different. Flat."

2. D Stanley waited for a long time before he spoke. "The thing is," he said, "I'm just not happy anymore. I'm tired of being flat. I want to be a regular shape again, like other people."

3. A He had found what he wanted—an old bicycle pump. He held it up, and Stanley and he looked at each other. "Okay," Stanley said at last. "But take it easy." He put the end of the long pump hose in his mouth and clamped his lips tightly about it so that no air could escape. "I'll go slowly," Arthur said. "If it hurts or anything, wiggle your hand at me." He began to pump.

4. B A moment more and he was all rounded out; head and body, arms and legs. But not his right foot. That foot stayed flat. Arthur stopped pumping. "It's like trying to do the very last bit of those long balloons," he said. "Maybe a shake would help." Stanley shook his right foot twice, and with a little *whooshing* sound it swelled out to match the left one.

5. C Everyone was terribly excited and happy, of course. Mrs. Lambchop made hot chocolate to celebrate the occasion, and several toasts were drunk to Arthur for his cleverness.

플랫 스탠리: 스탠리의 첫 번째 모험!
(Flat Stanley: His Original Adventure!)

1판 1쇄   2017년 9월 04일
2판 1쇄   2024년 4월 22일

지은이   Jeff Brown
기획   김승규
책임편집   김보경 정소이
콘텐츠제작및감수   롱테일 교육 연구소
저작권   명채린
마케팅   두잉글 사업 본부

펴낸이   이수영
펴낸곳   롱테일북스
출판등록   제2015-000191호
주소   04033 서울특별시 마포구 양화로 113, 3층(서교동, 순흥빌딩)
전자메일   help@ltinc.net

ISBN 979-11-91343-59-5 14740